949.3
L
LODER, DOROTHY
    Land and people of
    Belgium

DATE DUE			
APR 2			
NOV 17			
DEC 3			
DEC 5			
		.	
GAYLORD M-2			PRINTED IN U.S.A.

Loder 1212

THE LAND AND PEOPLE OF BELGIUM

The Land and People of

BELGIUM

BY DOROTHY LODER

PORTRAITS OF THE NATIONS SERIES

J. B. Lippincott Company

PHILADELPHIA AND NEW YORK

COPYRIGHT © 1957 BY DOROTHY LODER
PRINTED IN THE UNITED STATES OF AMERICA
LIBRARY OF CONGRESS CATALOG CARD NUMBER 57-6283
FIFTH PRINTING

For Arthur

CHAPTERS

THE LAND AND PEOPLE OF BELGIUM

1. THE CROSSROADS

BELGIANS are famous for their sense of humor. During World Wars I and II, they made dangerous fun of their German conquerors and their own misfortune; nowadays they quip about their air force and laugh at disputes between Flemish-speaking Belgians of the north and French-speaking Walloon Belgians of the south. They joke about their chilly, damp climate, ridicule judges, politicians and writers. Yet if you speak of "little Belgium," they are not amused.

They admit the area of the country is not great. Reaching from Germany and the Grand Duchy of Luxemburg west to the North Sea and from France north to Holland, it is smaller than Holland, less than a third the size of Portugal and only slightly larger than our state of Maryland. But they point out that this territory supports four times the population of Maryland, nearly as many people as Portugal and only a million less than Holland.

They tell how Belgian scenery changes from North Sea dunes and dikes to the gorges and forested hills of the Ardennes to the southeast. They list a dozen cities which contain so many historic buildings, such a wealth of painting, carving, sculpture as to be called art cities. They recall the nation's long roll of painters, writers, musicians, kings, crusaders and patriots.

Belgium has played an important, though tragic, part in history, too, chiefly because it lies without natural barriers at the crossroads of northwestern Europe. Century after century, invading armies have turned it into a battleground and military graveyard.

1

Near the old city of Tongres in the east, eight thousand Roman soldiers lie buried where, two thousand years ago, they fell fighting tribes of the region, those "Belgae" whom Julius Caesar described as "the fiercest of the Gauls." The two world wars of our own century scattered cemeteries of our allies everywhere: British in Flanders, French along the River Meuse and in the Ardennes. Thousands of Americans are buried in the Ardennes town of Bastogne, which was the key to the 1944 Battle of the Bulge.

Since the Middle Ages, Belgians have fought in wars not of their own making, have been robbed and oppressed; they have seen fields wasted, cities burned and looted. Yet when the smoke lifted and war ended, they replanted, rebuilt and went back to their hard-working, everyday lives. The farmer on his below-sea-level land, the artisan beating out copperware, cutting diamonds or weaving textiles, the miner bringing coal from the deepest and most dangerous mines in Europe, the small-town or big-city burgomaster (mayor) taking the duties of office so seriously are all typical of a people who have clung to their self-respect through centuries of misfortune.

It is surprising so much has survived the turmoil of the past or has been restored. At times, another age lingers on in a whole town, as in storybook Bruges, which looks much as in the sixteenth century. Often you catch a glimpse of long ago when you stand in some Grand' Place (Main Square), flanked by a cathedral, town hall, bell tower and splendid houses of the guilds or tradesmen's unions. The past reflects from the waters of a canal flowing between high, gabled houses. It lurks behind the ramparts of a crusader's castle, echoes in the chimes of ancient belfries.

Enemies found Belgium easy to invade. Peacetime visitors also discover it is easy to enter, for it is veined with rivers and canals, highways, railroads and interurban trolleys. Barges ply its waterways from France to the North Sea. Two great rivers, the Scheldt and the Meuse, rising in France, flow through Belgium to enter the North Sea from Holland. The Scheldt provides the Belgian seaports of Ghent and Antwerp. Farther to the east, the Meuse sweeps north between rocky white cliffs, wooded slopes, old towns and castles; it flows past Liège, a city rich in history and modern industry; then, beyond Liège, shunting its heavy barge traffic into the Albert Canal, which veers west to Antwerp, the Meuse swings along the Dutch-Belgian frontier and finally enters Holland.

The densest network of railroads in the world covers Belgium, with Brussels, the capital, at its center. International trains pass through Brussels en route to Germany, France, Holland; there is even a train and ferry service from Brussels direct to London. Air and steamship lines bring in travelers from the Americas, Africa and the rest of Europe, while helicopters connect Brussels with cities in Belgium, northern France, Holland and Germany.

The Belgian coast is slightly more than an hour from Brussels by train. This region of stormy, bitter winters can be delightful when summer winds blow over the high, golden dunes and tangle the long strands of *oyat* grass planted to hold down the sand. The forty-odd miles along the North Sea are strung with towns where in summer the flags of the nine provinces flap over beaches crowded with people from each province, as well as with foreign vacationers. In Ostend, perhaps the best known of the seaside resorts, visitors flock to the Casino, the theater, the race track, the beaches, while Ostend harbor goes about its everyday business—fishing. Fishermen sit on the shore mending nets, unload their slippery hauls on the docks, crowd the market where the catch is auctioned off, or prepare to put to sea again. Some vessels sail for waters off Scotland and Denmark, others, the big trawlers, for as far away as Iceland, a four-day voyage into the foggy North Atlantic, where they spend ten days catching haddock and cod.

Behind the North Sea dikes and dunes and along both banks of the Scheldt above Antwerp lie the polders. Polder land has been made of silt and sand deposited by the sea. Once the polders lay under water; they are still below sea level and are crisscrossed by ditches and canals which carry off water that would otherwise stand in the fields. In the polder country, roads run on causeways above meadows lush with grass. Fat black and white cattle graze in the meadows and vegetables grow in narrow fields. Poplars line the roads and canals, willows outline the fields, with here and there a stand of evergreens and a cluster of apple or pear trees shading the farm buildings, while now and again a windmill towers over the flat green land.

A few miles inland, the polder belt lifts to higher ground. Now the Flanders plain is scattered with towns and villages so near together you see steeple after steeple of village after village and hear their bells across the meadows. The fields of flax flower into blue lakes in June and July; the trees are heavier as they shade the farmhouses or outline the meanders of slow streams. Around Ghent, "the city of flowers," stretch acres of greenhouses where roses and orchids are raised, while begonias, azaleas and rhododendrons bloom in the open.

From the city of Antwerp east through the province of Limburg to the Dutch border reaches a district known as the Campine; it stretches out in mile upon mile of empty moors patched in yellow broom and purple heather, stitched by firs and pines, knotted with clumps of white birch. Grass for the cattle is sparse and many farms are small and poor. Much of the Campine has been wild and neglected and picturesque for a long time, but that is not so true now, for parts of it are becoming rich, crowded and ugly. Coal mines, discovered fifty years ago in Limburg, are being worked on a large scale, and as they are better than the old mines to the south around the cities of Mons, Charleroi and Liège, smelters, foundries, zinc works and other industries have followed them into the region.

But industry has not yet disfigured all the countryside. Southern Limburg is planted in orchards, and the month of May turns it into a sweet-smelling bouquet of apple, pear, plum and cherry blossoms. The cherry crop attracts buyers for preserve factories from as far away as England; the cherry festival in the Limburg town of Saint-Trond celebrates the harvest with decorated floats and giants paraded through the streets, a carnival on the Grand' Place and luscious cherry tarts served everywhere.

In Brabant, the grape growers claim they have perfect bunches ripe every day of the year. Their black grapes form on vines clustering under the glass of thousands of hothouses on the southern slopes southeast of Brussels. Red-roofed Brabantine towns around the capital, rising from the best farm land in Belgium, stand among billowing fields of wheat, barley, hops and sugar beets.

Brabant is also a country of forests, castles and battlefields. Only a short drive south from Brussels is Waterloo, with its monuments to the final defeat of Napoleon Bonaparte in 1815. The largest and most impressive of the memorials raised there is a pyramid of grassy earth, high as a hill, on which a mammoth bronze lion looks watchfully across the fields toward France.

Waterloo lies on an imaginary line traced east and west from the North Sea across to the German border which divides Belgium into two almost equal parts. This ancient and significant marker is called a linguistic frontier, because the inhabitants of the region above it speak Flemish, a language almost identical with Dutch, whereas below it, the natives speak French. The Flemish-speaking area of Belgium comprises not only the provinces of East and West Flanders, but also Antwerp, Limburg and part of Brabant, and all of it is referred to by the general term Flanders. The southern half of the country, or Wallonia, the territory of the Walloons, includes the French-speaking part of Brabant, plus the provinces of Hainaut, Namur, Liège and Luxemburg, not to be confused with the Grand Duchy of Luxemburg of which it was once a part. Although Brussels is situated in Flemish-speaking Brabant, most of its citizens speak both French and Flemish, as is proper in the capital of a bilingual nation.

Heavy industry has concentrated south of the linguistic frontier

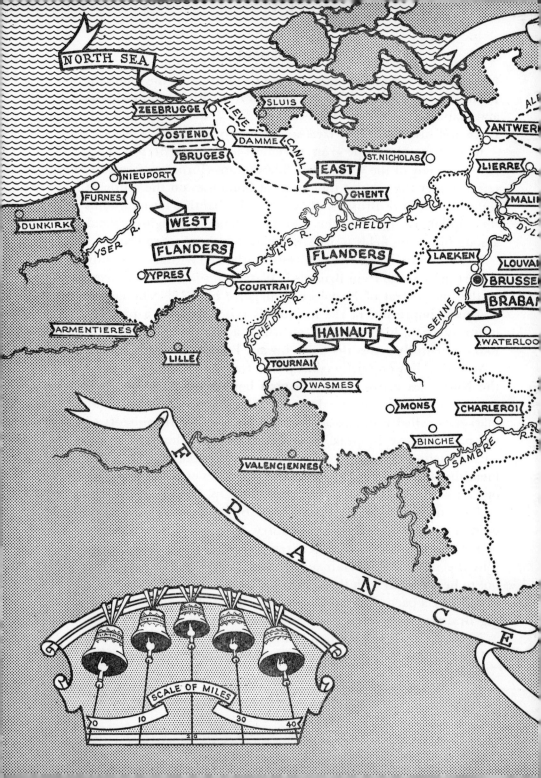

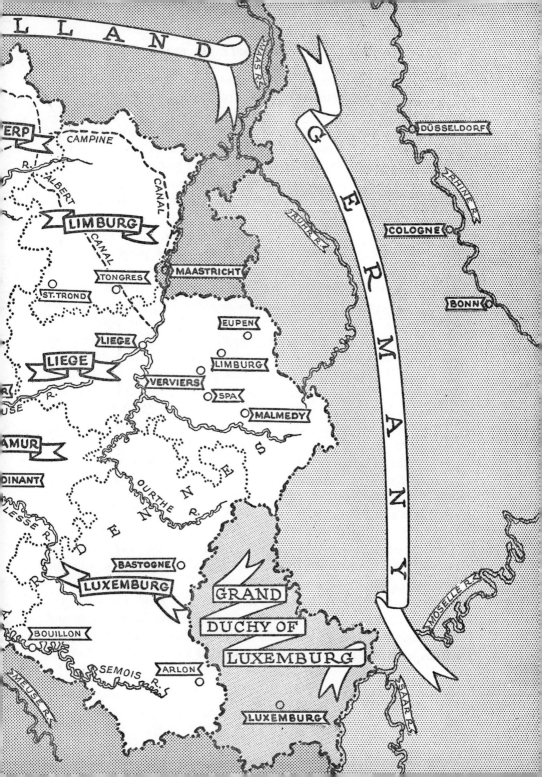

for generations. Here and there monstrous slag heaps disfigure the landscape and thick gray dust from stone quarries settles on the fields; factory chimneys smoke, forges and furnaces stain the damp air with their glow. Coal mines have blackened the region about the cities of Mons, Charleroi and Liège for centuries. These mines, worked regularly for three hundred years, are rapidly being stripped and grow increasingly dangerous. Abandoned portions near Liège have sunk so much that some districts of the city are threatened with cave-ins.

Nevertheless, the Walloon provinces are not all factory towns and grimy working-class settlements. In many places, they unroll mile after mile of scenery that grows wilder and lovelier as it climbs to the southeast. The Ardennes, a land of wooded hills, narrow valleys and wide green vistas extending through several southern and eastern provinces, seems far from the polders and plains. In its forests, hunters kill small game, stalk deer and shoot wild boar; now and again someone kills a wolf. Like the North Sea coast, the Ardennes is a summer playground for Belgium, a spot beloved by vacationers, who camp, hike, fish and drink the mineral waters which well up in springs throughout the region. The name of the town of Spa has become a word in the dictionary meaning a place where there are mineral springs. For centuries, Spa was the favorite resort of kings and queens, and to it came the great and rich of Europe. Of late, however, it has lost many of its fashionable visitors and most of the expensive hotels that catered to them have closed or changed into holiday inns for working people.

Rivers of the Ardennes have musical names like the Lesse, the Ourthe, the Semois, the Ninglinspo. On their way to join the Meuse, some tumble through ravines or leap in cascades; others meander widely; one or two carve caves. The Lesse has made the Caverns of Han, a fairy-tale palace glimmering in underground darkness. Tours of the caverns lead you through chambers with names such as The Alhambra, Boudoir of Proserpine, Hall of the

Dome, where stalactites hang like icicles from lofty ceilings and stalagmites heap up fantastic landscapes; you hear echoes beating against the cavern walls and ride the Lesse in a boat as it flows out from the caves into the light. Quite a different trip from one you may have taken a day or two earlier on a canal in Bruges!

2. THE FAMILY NAME
IS BELGIAN

IF YOU look at the Belgian coat of arms, you see one motto below the lion to the left and another under the lion at the right. Both mean "In Union there is Strength," but the words to your left, *"L'Union fait la Force"* are French, while at the right *"Eendracht maakt Macht"* says the same thing in Flemish. This double motto hints at the nation's problem of keeping peace between the French and Flemish-speaking Belgians who make up its nine million population in almost equal parts—there are slightly more Flemish than Walloons.

In theory, the two peoples may be contrasted in race, appearance, temperament and talents, as well as the language they speak. The typical Fleming, of Germanic stock, is sturdy, broad faced, blue eyed, with golden or reddish hair. Some are very handsome. There are also beautiful Walloons, who are usually darker, with clear skin and a smaller frame; sometimes they look Irish or Welsh. This resemblance is understandable, because Walloons, like the Irish and Welsh, descend from the Celts who spread in prehistoric times across Europe from the British Isles into Spain; the Flemish word *Waelsch,* meaning Walloon, comes from the same root as Welsh.

If you describe the Fleming, you write "thoughtful, pious, stubborn, conservative yet friendly and pleasure-loving, when angry, brutal." For the Walloon, you choose words such as "lively, gay, restless, cynical, friendly, yet ready to fight at the slightest excuse." Usually, the Belgian painters, sculptors and architects have been Flemings, the musicians were Walloons. Two Walloon names are familiar in the United States: César Franck, whose *Symphony in D Minor* is so often played, was born in the city of Liège; Adolphe Sax, from Dinant on the Meuse, made the first saxophone about a hundred and twenty years ago.

In the past, Flemings worked alone or in small groups at painstaking crafts handed down from one generation to the next, and to some extent they still are individual craftsmen. The women make lace and embroidery, the men fashion musical instruments and carve furniture—though now most furniture is machine-made, even in Flanders. Walloons do things on a larger scale. Rolling mills, foundries, quarries, glass works were almost all in Wallonia until a few years ago when some large plants were established in the coal mine district of the Campine.

Theoretically, Fleming and Walloon contrast sharply, but in fact it is often impossible to distinguish between them, since centuries of intermarriage have so blurred racial differences that the only real barrier dividing them remains that of language. French and Flemish are not in the least alike.

Flemish won full recognition as a second official language only about twenty-five years ago. French had reluctantly yielded it some place in government business before then, but was still heard in law courts, schools, offices, on the stage, at most social gatherings. The upper classes in Flanders spoke French as naturally as in Wallonia, their neglect of "the vulgar Netherlandish tongue," as they called Flemish, dating from the Middle Ages when France dominated the region, and nobles, churchmen and rich merchants associated with Frenchmen of similar rank and interests. Occasionally, in medieval times, even the Count of Flanders did not trouble to learn Netherlandish and could not communicate directly with his subjects, peasants and humble townspeople, who still spoke their native Germanic language.

The French of educated Walloons differs only in minor details from the French of France, yet Wallonia also cherishes a dialect, one that resembles Old French of a thousand years ago and contains many Germanic words. No literature of value has been written in this dialect for centuries, but learned societies have been formed to study "the language which has known better days." Amateur theatrical groups stage Walloon plays, mostly farces; students at Liège University pride themselves on their repertory of dialect songs which they sing when they gather in clubs and cafes. You might say that most Walloons have the dialect in their blood. A young Belgian whose family comes from the Ardennes but has lived for several generations in Brussels said: "We never speak anything but French at home unless my mother is angry; then she scolds us in Walloon."

When Belgium became an independent nation in 1830, French was declared the state language, even though the lower class in Flanders, more than half the nation's entire population, spoke Flemish. If you think it was unfair to ignore this speech of country districts and narrow back streets, remember that, although Flemish was written like Dutch, when spoken it broke into a jumble of dialects hard to understand from one community to the next. Such a confusion of languages would have been hard for the weak young Belgian government to cope with.

Yet the people clung to their speech, loving it as they loved Flanders. A few Flemish intellectuals, too, felt the injustice of subjecting citizens to laws and officials they could not understand. These men started the pro-Flemish or Flamingant movement. They began to write in Netherlandish, telling of the glories of Flanders in bygone days and demanding recognition for the language.

Some of the most ardent Flamingants had French names as, for example, Hendrik Conscience, who ignored the fact that his father was French and prized only the inheritance from his Flemish mother. His novel, *The Lion of Flanders,* retelling the fourteenth-century struggles of Flanders against France, thrilled the Flamingants. The book took its title from the black lion crouching on the coat of arms of the Counts of Flanders. A stirring old song, also entitled "The Lion of Flanders," became a hymn as dear to Flemings as the "Brabançonne," the Belgian national anthem.

Struggle for equality lasted nearly a century, since all injustices were not swept away until after World War I. In 1914, Flemish boys went into the army without knowing a word of French; they fought under officers who in many cases spoke only French. Hearing commands they did not understand, seeing in the trenches signs and directions printed only in French, these men grew confused, then resentful; finally, some of them openly hoped for German victory. These dangerous conditions were remedied as soon as the war ended, and ever since then the Belgian Army has contained separate French and Flemish units, so that a young man upon becoming a soldier may be assigned to an outfit where he hears his native tongue. All officers are supposed to speak both.

If you do not like language study, you must sympathize with a Belgian child. All schools, while using the speech of the district where they are situated, teach the second language. In Flanders, pupils drudge over French grammar and vocabulary in addition to their own Flemish. They have, by the way, learned to speak a more correct Netherlandish than their parents and grandparents, and with them the confusion of dialects is beginning, but just beginning, to disappear. If a child lives in the country or a small town in Wallonia and speaks dialect at home, he is even worse off, for he has two new languages to struggle with, French and Flemish. Finally, if he visits friends in the region around Arlon or Eupen and Malmédy he hears something else again—German! All this and German too in a country slightly larger than Maryland!

Although Brussels is north of the linguistic frontier in Flemish-speaking Brabant, most of its citizens know both languages. It would be more exact to say that almost everyone knows French,

because the Flemish, who outnumber Walloons in the city, speak
it with varying degrees of fluency—some perfectly, others badly.
As a rule, the working class in the capital is Flemish: the taxicab
drivers, policemen, shopkeepers need French to deal with wealth-
ier, French-speaking fellow-citizens, as well as with tourists. Walloons often know very little Flemish, and this seeming indifference
irritates the Flemings. It is said that if a Walloon asks a Fleming
a question in French he is likely to get a stupid stare for an answer.
However, the Fleming seems to be naturally better at languages
than most people; even an uneducated man is likely to pick up
English and German in addition to French. One Flemish waiter,
whose English was sufficient, boasted: "Give me a month and I
could learn to speak Chinese."

Several theaters in the capital produce Flemish plays, but many
more give works in French. Nine or ten daily papers in French
are for sale at the newsstands, as compared with six or seven in
Flemish. Of course, the city is officially bilingual: Trains are announced, street signs posted, names of business firms printed in
both languages. Yet it is French you hear at social affairs, business meetings, in smart restaurants and shops. Walloons complain
that Flemings are overbearing in their efforts to impose their
language, and both sides are always disputing about something.
Recently, the Flemings campaigned against the way in which
Brussels street cars posted the sign *Défense de fumer,* which is
French for "No Smoking," above the Flemish *Niet Roken.* They
protested so loudly that the street car company compromised by
letting half the trolleys keep *Défense de fumer* on top, while the
other half now carry it below *Niet Roken.*

Although you may be glad Flemish has come into its own, there
are times when you wish for a single Belgian language, as for instance when you are touring the country. If you are in Flanders
en route, say, to Mons, how are you to guess that "Bergen" on the
road signs is the city you want? Or that Luik is Flemish for Liège,
that Doornijk is Tournai, and Maas means Meuse? There is much

more of this national double talk, with now and then the English name thrown in for good measure. For example, the river we call the Scheldt is the Schelde in Flanders and the Escaut in Wallonia.

To judge only by the continual bickering between Flemings and Walloons, you might think Belgium hopelessly divided. Yet this split shows as a mere surface crack under pressure of danger to the nation. Then the two sides stop squabbling and unite against their common enemy. Both groups realize they are bound by many similar traits, by like ambitions as well as by hardships endured together; they remember their long struggle for freedom; they have one religious faith, for Belgium is almost entirely Roman Catholic. The Constitution has guaranteed freedom of worship since it went into force in 1831, and yet few Belgians are Protestants and the country has even fewer Jews.

Only a handful of Flamingants have agitated for an independent Flanders, or Flanders joined with Holland; most Flemings are devoted to the black, yellow and red Belgian flag, even though they make a great to-do over their black lion on the yellow standard of Flanders. The better you know Belgium and its people, the more you believe the often-quoted saying that"Flemish and Walloon are only given names; the family name is Belgian."

3. THE AIR OF THE TOWN
MAKES A MAN FREE

FLYING over Belgium, you see it as a green, black and silver fabric netted by rivers, canals, railroads and highways, embroidered thickly with villages, spotted by mines, quarries and smelters. When you think of the many and varied Belgian industries and recall that more people live here to the square mile than anywhere else in Europe except Holland, you find such words as rich, crowded, complicated to describe the land below you.

Belgian history, too, is rich and crowded; it is complicated by princely intrigues, claims to rulership based on royal marriages, ambition for land and power, commercial rivalries between cities and between nations, religious hatreds. Over the past thousand years, most of the wars of western Europe have raged across Flanders and Wallonia.

Yet, through the turmoil, the inhabitants of the region have kept their dreams of independence. Because they were not free, they valued freedom above everything else. Revolting again and again at the tyranny of their lords and the oppression of invaders, men died for liberty. Citizen rebellions were crushed, but gradually the rulers yielded a share of local self-government to the hardy, determined people. In the Middle Ages, men said, "The air of the town makes a man free," and it is true that the united strength of the townsmen won the first small rights to a share in local affairs.

The idea of self-government was born early in the Netherlands, as the area comprising both Belgium and Holland was called. Netherlands towns prospered in the dim past. They grew along a Roman road or on a navigable river near the sea, and their merchants, craftsmen and other workers built up a lively trade at home and abroad. As towns became larger, the citizens banded together according to their occupations into guilds or corporations; there was a bakers' guild; the weavers had a guild; the brewers formed a guild. Some cities counted as many as fifty-two different corporations, which regulated hours and working conditions for members, fixed pay and length of apprenticeship for those learning the trade, and fought for a voice in choosing town officials, in fixing taxes and in determining when the citizens should be called for military service.

The Crusades, which began at the end of the eleventh century, helped the towns and strengthened the guilds. Belgian princes, who flocked to rescue Jerusalem and the Holy Sepulcher from the Saracens, took armies of their followers with them, and to raise enormous sums needed to finance the long and costly expeditions, they not only disposed of lands and castles but also sold rights and privileges to towns on their estates.

The merchants and tradesmen often paid well for the lord's written promise never again to collect a certain heavy tax; they bought his permission to build a wall about their town so as to defend it better; they bargained for the right to raise a high bell tower. The burghers of the Netherlands considered a belfry as the symbol of liberty and thought whoever held the tower ruled the town. A city's charter of rights and all its valuable documents could be locked away behind the iron doors of a room at the base of the tower; the bells above, which warned of fire, flood and the approach of enemies, which summoned citizens to the public square to hear good news or bad, were the city's voices of anger, grief and joy.

The Latin inscription on one old bell reads: "I praise the true

God; I summon the people; I assemble the clergy; I mourn the dead; I put the plague to flight; I wail at the funeral; I abate the lightning; I proclaim the Sabbath; I arouse the lazy; I scatter the winds; I soften the cruel." If the people believed all these claims, they thought the bell had magical powers. Of course we do not know exactly what they did believe, but we are certain they regarded their bells with pride and affection; indeed, they still do. They gave names to the mighty ones—Roland was the big bell of Ghent; Karolus and Gabriel lorded it over the smaller bells in Antwerp.

As the towns bought and fought themselves free of the nobles, you might expect to hear they were governed in a democratic way. Usually, this was not true. When some burghers, like the merchants and brewers, for example, grew richer and more important than their fellow citizens, they assumed more than their share of authority. Powerful guilds, ignoring poorer corporations, refused them a voice in city affairs. Sometimes this attitude brought on civil war between the arrogant rich and the truculent poor; more than once, Ghent, Bruges, Ypres and other cities saw their own men cut each others' throats in class fighting.

The most famous quarrel of this kind developed into a thrilling story which ended with the Battle of the Golden Spurs, so well described in Hendrik Conscience's novel, *The Lion of Flanders.* When the aristocrats of Bruges became too overbearing, the Count of Flanders sided with the poorer people against them. Enraged, the aristocrats turned for support to King Philip the Fair of France. The French king was delighted at an excuse for meddling in Flemish affairs and sent armed help to the *Leliaerts,* or Men of the Lily, as the king's party called themselves because of the lily on the banners of France. The workers, on the other hand, rallied about the Count of Flanders, calling themselves the *Clauwaerts,* or Men of the Lion's Claw, from the lion on their lord's coat of arms.

Philip invaded Flanders, defeated the Clauwaerts, took the

Count prisoner and raised the French fleur-de-lis over Bruges where the lion's banner had lately waved; he believed he had won the city. But he did not know how to deal with his new subjects, for he immediately levied new taxes; the Flemish detested (and still detest) taxes of all kinds. To make things worse, he garrisoned the town with French soldiers whose insolence infuriated the citizens.

Now, when the French entered Bruges, they had failed to capture five thousand of the principal Clauwaerts, who had fled to nearby towns and farms. As discontent grew within the city and news spread abroad that it was ready to revolt, a son of the Count of Flanders plotted its delivery with two of the escaped Clauwaerts leaders, Pieter de Coninc, a weaver, and the butcher, Jan Breydel. We hear little about Jan, but a great deal about Pieter, who, though a frail and sickly man with only one eye, was a born leader able to inspire his comrades with his own courage.

Just before dawn one summer morning, he led the Clauwaerts back into Bruges through breaches the French had made in the city walls. Inside the city, they were joined by Clauwaerts sympathizers; the combined force struck suddenly and savagely. They fell upon the French. Any man who could not say "Shield and Friend" in Flemish with a Flemish accent was considered a Frenchman and killed without mercy. This slaughter is known as the Matins of Bruges, because it took place early in the morning—too pretty a name for such an ugly dawn.

When word of the Matins reached King Philip, he swore revenge and began gathering together an army of his best knights. The Clauwaerts were not frightened, nor did they shrink from the battle they knew must be fought. Instead, they appealed to all the neighboring towns for help. Ypres sent twelve hundred men, "five hundred dressed in scarlet, seven hundred dressed in black;" seven hundred marched out from Ghent, while other volunteers came from as far away as Liège. On July 11, 1302, near

Courtrai, south of Bruges, the Clauwaerts and their allies met the splendor of Philip's chivalry.

What happened was almost unbelievable. The Clauwaerts were on foot except for some thirty mounted knights attending the son of the Count of Flanders; Philip's army consisted of superbly armed horsemen reinforced by a body of crossbowmen from Genoa in Italy. The Clauwaerts wore no armor except iron helmets; they carried heavy pikes as their only weapons. Yet they held against the French onslaught, standing with pikes fixed firm as an iron wall. The French charge, having been too hasty, broke against the pikes, and the horses scattered and stumbled in the marshy earth, dragging down their heavily armored riders. Seeing the confusion, the Flemish rushed upon the enemy and killed without quarter. When the battle was over, de Coninc's soldiers took seven hundred pairs of golden spurs from the feet of knights lying dead on the field. They gave the spurs to the church of Notre Dame in Courtrai, where they hung for many years. You may visit Notre Dame in Courtrai, for it has survived wars that destroyed so much else in the city, but you look in vain for the golden spurs, and no one can tell you what became of them.

It is a shame the story of this victory does not end: "And Flanders lived happy ever after." However, as history rarely works out so neatly, the best we can say here is: "After Courtrai, Flanders kept the French at bay for twenty years." Then France prevailed and the Flemish took up their hard struggle for independence. Soon the Netherlands were involved in the Hundred Years War between France and England.

England was Flanders' friend. If you look at the map, you see why. London, on the Thames, lies directly across the North Sea from the mouth of the Scheldt. For centuries, trade with inland Europe, flowing through the Netherlands by river, canal and road to port cities like Bruges, came on over the narrow strip of sea to London. The English realized that safe, open Flemish ports favored their own commerce; that their prosperity depended on the

thousands of pounds of English wool which the Flemish weavers
bought and made into cloth so fine in texture and quality it was
sold as far away as Russia and Denmark. For their part, the Flemish saw their best hope of shaking off French rule in help from
this neighbor and business associate which also hated France.

Nevertheless, when King Edward III of England claimed the
French throne in 1340, the people of Flanders tried to remain neutral in the Hundred Years War brought on by his demands. The
King of France agreed to respect their neutrality—and then immediately broke his promise. Realizing they must take sides, the
Flemish followed the lead of Jacques van Artevelde, an influential
brewer of Ghent, who offered his city's help to the English king.
Edward came to Flanders—you see the ruins of Saint Bavon's Mon-
astery in Ghent, where he lived while plotting his campaign
against the French.

At first, Edward's plans went well. Leading his fleet of three
hundred vessels in a raid up the river Zwyn, he attacked eight
hundred French ships anchored off the town of Sluis and won a
smashing victory. Today, you can go over that battle site without
walking on water, for Sluis, just across the Belgian frontier in
Holland, now is an inland town! In the century after Edward's
victory, tides so completely silted up the Zwyn that polder fields
replaced sea water about Sluis. Deep, deep down in polder mud
lie rotted ship hulks, and rust that used to be weapons. If you
could dig far enough, perhaps you might find gold and silver coins,
sailors' medals and charms, even a gold chain or ring or a jeweled
sword hilt embedded in the silt.

Sluis was the only British success in so many years that Flanders
lost heart and King Edward went home to England. In Ghent,
van Artevelde's enemies turned on him and murdered him. Flanders' share of the Hundred Years War proved to be destruction,
disease and death.

The war brought ruin of another kind, because when Edward
left, some of the best Flemish weavers followed him to England,

where they taught their craft to the English, who thereafter, made their own wool into cloth, while the weavers in Flanders had to buy Spanish wool, a product so harsh and inferior that all the Flemish skill could not turn it into the fine material of earlier days. Gradually, England captured the woolen goods trade in Europe, and cities like Ghent, Ypres, Courtrai had to begin making linen from the flax which grew, and still grows, in fields about Courtrai. However, in the Campine, the textile cities did not find any industry to substitute; the looms stood idle; weavers and dyers drifted away in search of work; the towns dwindled into the villages we see today, each huddled about a church too large and handsome for such an insignificant place.

4. THE GRAND DUKES
OF THE WEST

BRUGES, GHENT and the other Flanders cities were not the only ones to struggle for liberty and power. Although Flanders developed earlier than the rest of the country, the history of most of the Netherlands tells of towns growing rich and self-reliant, burghers wresting individual liberty from their overlords and poor workers fighting for and winning equality with the important citizens. Only in the Ardennes was the story different, because the Ardennes, with few towns, peasants living like serfs among the forests, and robber lords in fortress castles, seemed centuries behind the times.

By the middle of the fourteenth century, not only were the inhabitants of the province of Brabant protected by charters guaranteeing their rights and privileges, but they were also busy and successful. The city of Brussels, though not so splendid as Bruges or Ghent, flourished. Brussels-made armor glinted in tournaments throughout Europe; Brussels tapestry hung in castles from Scandinavia to Spain; kings, princes, churches bought the work of Brussels gold and silversmiths.

Dinant, one of "the twenty-two good towns" of the bishopric of Liège, was making fine beaten brass and copper as early as the tenth century; these *dinanderies* of medieval times, crosses, candlesticks, baptismal fonts and even statues of copper, were treasured at home and abroad. Verviers, another of the good towns wove textiles by 1300—it still is an important woolen-mill town. Artisans and craftsmen of the city of Liège turned out handsome weapons and forged iron objects. Today the guns and locomotives manufactured in Liège are a great source of Belgian riches.

Even before the Battle of the Golden Spurs, the workers of Liège had forced from the bishop who was their ruling prince, the right to join churchmen and the nobles in making laws and fixing taxes for the province. They kept this privilege by fighting the nobles as well as the bishop, and year after year, class struggles tore the city with murders, revenges, wholesale massacres and the destruction of property. Then in the fifteenth century the artisans and nobles faced a common enemy—the Dukes of Burgundy, who, absorbing the Netherlands through marriage, military conquests and the purchase of territory, hoped to weld their lands into a monarchy. They called themselves the Grand Dukes of the West, but dreamed of being kings of the heart-land of Europe. Their ruthlessness and cruelty almost achieved this ambition, because they did not hesitate to do away with local privileges or use force to gain more power for themselves. When Ghent and Bruges rebelled at interference in city matters by Duke Philip the Good, he besieged both cities and executed the leaders of the uprisings. When Dinant rebelled in the last years of his reign, his son Charles the Bold sacked and burned the place, destroyed its town hall and cathedral and ordered eight hundred citizens, tied two together, drowned in the Meuse.

The story of Liège is more savage yet. If you have read Sir Walter Scott's novel, *Quentin Durward*, or seen the movie based on it, you remember how wily King Louis XI of France distrusted Charles the Bold, who was his vassal. Charles, for his part, loathed doing homage to Louis, and longed to be a king, too, and independent. The Liégeois also feared and hated Charles for his meddling in their affairs. Liège had been free as Burgundy for five hundred years; where Burgundy owed allegiance to France, Liège paid homage to the German emperor. Nevertheless, Charles was determined to annex the province.

Seeing a chance to turn Charles' quarrel with Liège to his own advantage, King Louis sent undercover agents to the people with promises of money and arms if they would defy the duke. The Liégeois attempted several small uprisings, which Charles punished severely. Then they attacked the bishop, Charles' cousin, who had been forced on them by the Burgundians. However, their timing was bad—they chose the very moment when Louis happened to be visiting Charles in his castle of Peronne. When news of the fracas, in which the bishop had not been hurt, reached Peronne, along with information about Louis' troublemaking, Charles told his royal guest he was a prisoner and would remain so until he agreed to join an expedition against Liège. Louis quickly agreed.

News of the approaching French-Burgundian army sent the chief citizens of Liège and the leading rebels scurrying into the Ardennes, leaving behind the poor, the old, and women and children in hopes the duke would spare them as harmless. The bishop himself rode out to meet his cousin and the king to beg mercy for the city, but they would not listen to him. Once inside Liège, Charles ordered its inhabitants killed, so many a day, and the city looted, then destroyed, so much of it every day. About fifty thousand Liégeois died in their ruined homes or were thrown into the Meuse to drown, while all buildings except churches were burned or torn down. Even in the brutal fifteenth century, the fate of Liège shocked Europe.

Yet in spite of such instances of tyranny and cruelty, Burgundian rule is the glory of early Netherlands history. For the first time, the country was almost united; never had it been more respected abroad, or richer. All Europe bought its textiles, tapestry, lace, weapons, gold and enamel wares, beaten copper, forged iron. Ships sailing up the River Zwyn unloaded on the wharves of Damme, the port of Bruges, cargoes of English tin, lead and cheese,

German wine, Spanish and Portuguese figs, olives, oranges and lemons. Cloth of gold came from Italy, furs from Russia, rugs from the Middle East, horses from Denmark, lions, monkeys and parrots from Africa. Merchants and bankers from seventeen foreign countries lived in Bruges in homes luxurious as palaces; the feasts and pageants of the nobles and rich merchants made society news for all Europe.

The Dukes of Burgundy kept more splendid state than any kings. Their court shone with storybook chivalry. In 1429, to commemorate his marriage with the Portuguese princess Isabella, Philip the Good founded the Order of the Golden Fleece, which somewhat resembles the Order of the Garter, established a hundred years earlier by King Edward III of England. For centuries afterwards, kings and princes of Europe coveted the honor of being a Knight of the Golden Fleece and proudly wore its jewel-studded golden chain or broad red ribbon, from which hung a small golden figure of a sheep.

When you are in Brussels, buying carnations and roses for sale on the Grand' Place, look about this vast public square. It was laid out in Burgundian times as a site for tournaments; hundreds of armed knights have jousted here to honor a ducal wedding or the birth of a duke's child. Lift your eyes to the figure of Saint Michael glittering from the spire of the Brussels town hall. The spire and Saint Michael rose up from the Grand' Place into the sky during the reign of Philip the Good.

His reign was the beginning of an age when religious orders, nobles, guilds and rich tradesmen vied with each other in building monasteries, churches, mansions and town halls; but beyond all the others, Philip, and after him his son Charles, lavished wealth and honors on artists. The dukes commissioned buildings, statues, paintings, gold and silver work; they ordered costumes designed, scenery and decorations made for the pageants which marked every Burgundian festival. It seems natural that Flemish painting should flower in Philip's reign, and proper to associate the last two great dukes, Philip and Charles, with the Flemish painters who, immortalizing the quiet Flanders landscape and the faces and figures of their fellow citizens, produced some of the world's masterpieces.

Duke Philip sent the painter Jan van Eyck to Portugal with the diplomats who arranged the duke's marriage to the Princess Isabella; it is probable that the artist's portrait of the lady gave Philip his first idea of what she looked like. You see van Eyck's work in Antwerp, Bruges and Ghent, but particularly in Ghent, where a small chapel of Saint Bavon's Cathedral contains the *Adoration of the Mystic Lamb,* considered one of the five or six greatest pictures in existence. Jan's shadowy brother Hubert is supposed to have begun the painting, but Jan, the younger by twenty years, finished it after Hubert's death. This twelve-paneled altarpiece has gone through a series of mystery-story adventures, for sections of it have been stolen more than once, only to be recovered. Only one panel has completely disappeared. Napoleon's soldiers carried off the central panel to Paris, where it hung in the Louvre until his downfall. Thieves made away with six side pieces that were sold and resold until finally the King of Prussia bought them for the Berlin Art Gallery; the peace treaty signed after World War I provided for their return to Ghent. When World War II threatened, the Belgian Government sent the altarpiece to Southern France for safety. However, when France fell, the Vichy regime gave the painting to the Nazis, although there was no need to do so, since it was in the unoccupied part of France. The Nazis took it off to Germany and after the war it turned up with other missing art treasures in a salt mine in Austria. Now, with one original panel missing, it has come home to Saint Bavon's. A panel has been substituted for the lost original and only an art expert would know it is not genuine.

You need not try to interpret the religious meaning of the work to enjoy its beauty, but you will have a hard time believing that the graceful figures and the enchanting backgrounds were painted five hundred years ago, so fresh and brilliant are the colors.

Although German-born, Hans Memling is considered a Flemish master, because he lived and worked most of his life in Bruges. Like van Eyck, Memling portrayed people and scenes with child-like, yet realistic clarity; his coloring, too, has kept its freshness. However, he surpasses van Eyck and the other artists of his time in religious feeling and imagination, in his gift for enchantment. Memling's greatest works are in Saint John's Hospital in Bruges. Among them is a portrait of Martin Nieuwenhoven, who seems to have been an important burgher of the town, though far from its handsomest. Martin's nose is big, his features heavy, and the bluish-gray velvet and wool suit he wears emphasizes the sallow-ness of his complexion. You would not say that he has an inter-esting face, and yet, as he prays, he really looks as though he sees a vision—the vision of the Madonna painted as a companion work to his portrait. The picture of Martin Nieuwenhoven is not Mem-ling's masterpiece, but it shows how he could mirror a man's soul.

Roger van der Weyden, a third artist of the Flemish school, was a Walloon who lived in Bruges (where he was Memling's teacher) and later settled in Brussels. As the painters he worked with were Flemish, he translated his French name, Roger de la Pasture into its Flemish equivalent and became Roger van der Weyden. In his religious pictures, the Blessed Virgin and the saints look like dignified Netherlanders posed against rich tapestries near stained-glass windows opening on Netherlandish scenery—river or canal, battlements, turrets and gabled roofs. You feel their human quality more than their saintliness.

Van der Weyden also painted the great men of his day, among others Philip the Good and Charles the Bold, and these portraits are priceless character sketches. When you see Charles as the artist saw him, you understand the fears of King Louis and the hatred of Liège. How arrogantly Charles wears the chain of the Golden Fleece! He holds his sword hilt with long, stiff fingers and glares at you with scorn. Gazing at him, you recall how his impatience and harshness undid all his father had accomplished toward uniting the Netherlands; you believe he loved war for its own sake, and feel a foreshadowing of his terrible fate: He fell in a winter battle before Nancy in France and when, days later, his followers found his body among the dead, it had been half devoured by wolves.

Charles' daughter Mary inherited the duchy at nineteen. With enemies harrying her on every side, she quickly married the man she thought best able to defend her lands, a German prince named Maximilian. Later on, Maximilian became an emperor, ruler of the Holy Roman Empire, a confederation of European states, but he could not keep peace with the Netherlands cities or with France, especially after Mary's death a few years following her marriage. The greatness of the Netherlands was over; less than half a century after the death of Charles the Bold, it became a Spanish possession when it was inherited by another Charles, the grandson of Mary and Maximilian.

This Charles acquired the throne of Spain through his mother's parents, King Ferdinand and Queen Isabella; the Netherlands came to him from his father, the son of Mary and Maximilian. Born in Ghent and brought up in the city of Malines, Charles preferred his native land to his mother's country when he was young, but as he grew older he took more interest in Spain and in the affairs of the Empire, where he succeeded Maximilian as ruler; he is usually called Charles V because he was the fifth emperor of the name. As the years went by, the Spaniards almost forgave him for being a "foreigner," but his popularity faded in the Netherlands; his own city of Ghent revolted against him and later on even replaced his statue with one to the murdered Jacques van Artevelde.

Charles was ostentatious like his Burgundian ancestors; he also had his great-grandfather Charles' passion for war, wasting much of his life and too much of his people's resources on the Burgundian feud with France. Endless campaigns and a restless life made him old by the time he was fifty-five. Knowing he had not long to live, he came back from Spain, thin as a skeleton, dressed in mourning black, and in a simple ceremony in the royal palace on the hill above Brussels turned over rule of the Netherlands to his son Philip.

5. THE SPANISH NETHERLANDS

WHILE the Netherlands chafed under the rule of Charles V, they had even more cause for discontent under his son Philip II, because Philip thought only of Spain and treated the Netherlanders like conquered people. Charles' wars had dragged them deep into debt; Philip demanded still more taxes for further wars. Charles had curbed the independence of several cities, but Philip's policy was to destroy all individual liberty and gather power to himself.

Charles set up the Inquisition in the Netherlands; Philip kept the Inquisitors busy. The Protestant Reformation, as it spread through the Netherlands, had made converts in both the northern and southern provinces; Philip believed the Inquisition could drive these converts back into the Catholic Church or so punish them as to frighten others away from the new faith. He urged and encouraged the Inquisitors to try anyone suspected of differing in thought, word or deed from Catholic teachings. As a result, thousands of men and women were condemned to heavy punishment or death for their beliefs.

Philip underestimated the independent spirit of the Netherlands, for Protestantism continued to grow. Thousands of converts fled to England, Germany, Sweden, but even more remained at home to riot and rebel against oppression. They wrecked churches and convents, smashed statues and stained glass, burned wood carvings, slashed and burned paintings. Philip's reply to their fierce disobedience was just as fierce. He sent the Duke of Alva from Spain to restore order. Alva, a ruthless soldier, brought bloodshed and horror to the country. Sometimes his soldiers massacred the inhabitants of an entire village in reprisal for an attack on a Spanish soldier. His court, called the Council of Blood, tried and sentenced to death on the least pretext; men were hanged for failure to pay exorbitant taxes.

Such brutality brought on rebellion and then plunged the country into open civil war. The leader of the opposition was Prince William of Orange, a nobleman who had been devoted to Charles V. At first, Prince William may not have planned to shake off Spanish rule, but may have hoped, rather, to make Philip behave with more humanity and justice, and in this movement he had the support of all the Netherlanders. However, religious disputes soon divided his followers. In the north, which had become solidly Protestant, people refused to let their Catholic allies worship in their territory, while those inhabitants who chose to remain in the southern provinces were just as stubbornly Catholic. When William declared himself a Protestant about twelve years after the outbreak of war, his Catholic followers in the south gave up the fight and accepted Philip's offer to soften his policies. The seven provinces of the Protestant north, however, refused to make peace with the king and fought on. Their struggle lasted for thirty more years until, at last, in the early seventeenth century, they were recognized as the free nation of Holland.

The Southern Netherlands, that is, the area corresponding to modern Belgium, waited two hundred years before achieving independence. For half of that time, they remained a Spanish possession. Considering Spain's long occupation, Belgium shows surprisingly few Spanish traits. Houses with dark, Spanish-tiled roofs can be seen in Brussels and Antwerp and at Furnes in Flanders, the most Spanish of all Belgian towns; now and then a Belgian has dark Spanish eyes, shining black hair and finely chiseled features; one or two customs exist that may perhaps be traced back to Spanish times. That is all, except for several festivals, notably the Carnival at Binche and the Procession of the Penitents at Furnes.

Binche has gone mad at Carnival time ever since 1549, when Charles V happened to be visiting his sister at her castle in the town. She arranged a celebration in honor of the recent Spanish conquest of Peru. The plumes and gaudy costumes of the *Gilles* of Binche are supposed to make the wearers look like the Incas of Peru. Every man in the town aspires to be a Gille or player, a member of the association which stages the carnival; every small boy longs to wear one day their heavily padded, embroidered costume with a cap from which tower ostrich plumes, to walk to the jingling of bells sewed on his suit.

The Gilles take over Binche for three days beginning on the Sunday before Mardi Gras and ending as Lent dawns. They parade down streets hung with red and yellow Spanish flags and littered with red and yellow confetti trailing from upper windows. Lower windows of shops and houses along the line of march have been boarded up against the barrage of oranges which the Gilles throw as they go, oranges that flatten on house fronts, spatter the streets and plop against the bodies of unlucky spectators. Yet this golden threat is forgotten in the excitement of hurdy-gurdy and viola music, the rhythm of wooden shoes click-clacking on the cobbles, the smell of bonfires sharp in the winter air. When the final procession reaches the Main Square on Mardi Gras evening, paraders and spectators circle in a wild dance. Later on come fireworks; still later, the Gilles and their guests dance at a masked ball. No wonder the Carnival at Binche is supposed to have given us our slang term "binge."

The Procession of the Penitents at Furnes is a different affair. As you watch its floats depicting religious scenes, its marchers acting out Bible stories as they go by, and especially when the penitents pass you, you recall gloomy medieval ideas of sin and atonement. Some of these black-robed penitents, their heads and faces swathed in a black hood, walk barefoot over the cobbles; each carries a heavy cross in repentance for some sin he has committed. The lovely Spanish town hall of Furnes, the gabled houses with blue and red tiled roofs have witnessed this somber show for three hundred years, and they lend it a chilling reality, a sense of the past which overcomes you. However, no sooner is the last parader out of the way than the crowds forget the awe with which they have watched the pious spectacle and begin milling around the booths of a fair set up in the market place. The town's gloomy mood vanishes; you scarcely believe that only a little while ago you were watching a drama of grief and repentance instead of this gay carnival scene.

Perhaps Belgium shows so little Spanish influence because comparatively few Spaniards came to the Netherlands. The armies Spain sent into the country comprised Italians, Germans, French and other Europeans hired to fight in Europe while Spaniards themselves went off to explore, exploit and colonize the New World. These hired soldiers were usually disreputable fellows who drank, brawled, robbed, bullied and were hated and avoided wherever they went. King Philip's promise to withdraw them was one concession which helped to pacify the Southern Netherlands.

Soon after Philip's death, his daughter the Archduchess Isabella and her husband, Archduke Albert, came to rule the Southern Netherlands. The people liked Isabella, so merry and kind-hearted, so unlike her somber father; they respected the thin, solemn Albert's efforts to govern justly. This couple brought with them the happiest years, the most nearly peaceful time in the history of the Spanish Netherlands. The country would have been truly prosperous had it possessed a good seaport, but Ostend was its only outlet to the sea, and not only was Ostend inferior to Bruges and Antwerp as a harbor but it was also held by the Northern Netherlands for some years before Archduke Albert could retake it.

Bruges had ceased to be a great port by the middle of the fifteenth century. Do you recall how Sluis, which witnessed King Edward III's naval victory over the French, became an inland town through the silting of the River Zwyn? As the same Zwyn had provided Bruges with its port, the same filling-in which shut Sluis away from the water also isolated Bruges until the once-rich maritime city looked over the polders instead of the masts of ships.

When vessels could no longer reach its wharves or those of Damme, which served as its port for a time, the merchants and bankers moved to Antwerp fifty miles up the winding Scheldt. Antwerp not only inherited Bruges' trade but increased it, to become the greatest port in Europe. Then, after a century's prosperity, it died, too—but not of silt. Antwerp was a war casualty. The story of its ruin is long and involved, but in brief, the struggle between Spain and the Northern Netherlands for possession of the city ruined it. The port was blocked during the latter part of the sixteenth century. When peace finally came, Holland held the land on both sides of the Scheldt between Antwerp and the sea, thus controlling traffic in and out, and refused to reopen the river to the Southern Netherlands. Not a ship moved between Antwerp and the North Sea for two hundred years.

Yet despite the loss of its riches, the city kept its prestige as a center of art and learning. Scholars and scientists were familiar sights in its narrow streets, in squares like the Glove Market, the Cobblers' Market and especially in the Friday Market where Christopher Plantin's house stood at the corner of Holy Ghost Street. Plantin, the best of Antwerp's printers, became one of the best in Europe. The friend as well as the publisher of learned men, he brought out their writings in volumes that were works of art. After Plantin's death, the firm continued under his son-in-law, Jan Moretus. Now it often used as illustrations the etchings of an Antwerp artist, Peter Paul Rubens.

Rubens is the outstanding member of a group of Flemish painters whose works, like those of van Eyck, Memling and their

contemporaries, are still admired and treasured. He was the in-
spiration of his fellow artists and might be said to have founded a
school of painting, yet he emerges most clearly not from a comparison with his followers but by contrast with a painter who died
eight years before he was born. This man was Pieter Brueghel.
Both Brueghel and Rubens are typically Flemish, but they are
very different. Brueghel painted during the years of the Civil
War; Rubens knew the happier early seventeenth century. In
spite of a long life spent in Brussels, Brueghel remained a peasant
at heart; Rubens was court painter for the Archduchess Isabella,
a friend of kings, nobles and scholars, something of a scholar himself and a top-flight diplomat. Brueghel depicted the life of peasants and plain people; Rubens painted aristocrats, and his work
pleased the most sophisticated critics. Brueghel is humorous, wry,
cynical; Rubens, urbane, lavish and charmed with the society he
knows. Each man represents the time and class to which he belonged.

Brueghel is more the historian than Rubens. The scenes he re-
corded with his brush give as true an account of his friends as if
he had used pen and paper to write about them. He brings to
life guests at a country wedding feast, harvesters resting in a field
of yellow wheat, peasants dancing, children stealing bird's nests.
To this day, the Flanders landscape seems waiting for him to paint
again with his precise outlines its feathery trees and swelling fields
of grain. The woman delivering milk, the taxicab driver, the fat
man dozing on a park bench might all be just about to pose for
him.

Brueghel's genius is individual; no other artist was like him.
Rubens, too, has a style peculiarly his own, even though he taught
young painters, many of whom were influenced by his genius. He
painted in the grand manner, with freedom, strength and a mas-
tery of color which delighted his own age and still impress artists
and critics. The great of Europe sat to him for portraits; when
Isabella sent him to Spain on a diplomatic mission, the king and

his grandees commissioned him to do forty portraits; the Queen of France ordered twenty-one enormous pictures to commemorate the chief events of her life. Two of his finest portraits, hanging in the Museum of Ancient Art in Brussels, are of Albert and Isabella. Albert is shown in profile, a thin, severe man. Isabella, plump and elderly, dressed in black with a white ruff and ropes of pearls, looks tired and worried yet amiable.

Rubens' masterpiece is not a portrait, however, but *The Descent from the Cross,* a religious painting in the cathedral of Antwerp, a scene which shows the apostles taking the dead Christ from the cross. Art critics speak of the body of Christ in this work as the finest human figure ever painted; the grouping of the other figures is superb, while tenderness and grief on every face and in every attitude draw you into the tragedy—a human rather than a divine tragedy.

Rubens possessed untiring energy. When not abroad on some mission for the Archduchess, he spent his days at home painting at top speed—he once completed a picture without any help in ten days—making designs for stained glass windows or for Brussels tapestries, engraving illustrations to be reproduced in the Plantin-Moretus books, remodeling his beautiful house in Antwerp, listening to someone read aloud from a scholarly book, or criticizing the work of his pupils. He ran the art school somewhat like a factory, organizing a production line when orders poured in too fast for him to fill alone. First he planned and sketched out the work as he wanted it to be; some of these sketches and tiny paintings are exquisite. Then he turned his plans over to his pupils, who blocked in the canvas, painted figures and faces. Since no picture left the studio until he had corrected and retouched it, each of the hundreds of signed Rubens canvases reflect his love of lavish outlines and luscious color, his genius for portraying rosy, exquisite flesh.

While Anthony van Dyck studied under Rubens, he used to paint the most difficult parts of these cooperative pictures, because the master realized the young man's rare talent. In his short life, van Dyck became a fashionable portrait painter; he did not bring out in his subjects the reality and individuality you see in Rubens' portraits, but he made his sitters look as aristocratic and handsome as they imagined or wished they were. Most of his works are in England, where he spent the last years of his life, but Brussels and his native Antwerp own a few. A number of museums in the United States also have some good van Dycks, as well as paintings by Rubens and a few works of fifteenth-century masters such as Jan van Eyck, van der Weyden and Memling.

Belgian Government Information Center

A peaceful summer scene in the Ardennes

Belgian National Tourist Office

The historic church of Saint Gudule in Brussels

Belgian Government Information Center

Le pont de Fragnée in the industrial city of Liège

A view of the crowded port of Antwerp

Belgian National Tourist Office

Belgian Government Information Center

An old windmill in Flanders

Belgian Government Information Center

One of the giants of the open-air festival at Ath

Belgian National Tourist Office

The famous lion of Waterloo, commemorating the defeat of Napoleon in 1815

Belgian Government Information Center

A lacemaker of Bruges

Belgian Government Information Center

The castle of Beersel, between Brussels and Malines

Belgian National Tourist Office

Children and donkeys on the sands at Knokke-sur-Mer

Belgian National Tourist Office

Le Quai Vert in the lovely old city of Bruges

Belgian Government Information Center

The house of Erasmus van Rotterdam at Anderlecht

Belgian National Tourist Office

Modern traffic and historic monuments on a busy Ghent street

Belgian Government Information Center

A whitewashed Walloon farmhouse

Belgian Government Information Center

The Castle of the Counts of Flanders

Belgian National Tourist Office

A view of the Brussels Grand'Place

Belgian Government Information Center

A farm near Ecaussines

6. THE VERY COCKPIT
OF CHRISTENDOM

IF Albert and Isabella had had a son to inherit the Southern Netherlands, the history of the land might have been happier. However, as they were childless, the provinces reverted to the King of Spain when Albert died in 1621. Isabella acted as regent for the twelve years she survived her husband. By the middle of the seventeenth century, the country was plunged again into Spain's endless wars with France, England and Holland. There was scarcely a Belgian field that enemy soldiers did not trample, hardly a village or town escaping pillage and damage. If you know the names of celebrated European battles of the time, you find most of them on a map of Belgium and realize what an Englishman meant when he wrote: "The Netherlands have been for many years the very cockpit of Christendom."

At the beginning of the eighteenth century, a French prince and an Austrian archduke fought for the Spanish throne, which had been left vacant by the death of the last direct heir. At war's end, the archduke had lost Spain but won the Southern Netherlands as a consolation prize. Austria kept the territory for eighty years, a time during which it did not fare badly. Nevertheless, the end of the century found the inhabitants restless and dissatisfied.

This was probably because revolution was the political fashion of the moment. The United States had recently won independence from England; the French Revolution was shaking Europe with its thunder, and clouds of discontent, drifting across the Continent, hung over Belgium. When the well-meaning but tactless Emperor Joseph II of Austria tried to tell his Netherlands subjects exactly what to think and how to live, they resented his interference; when he tried to change the way in which Catholic priests were educated, the storm burst. Imitating Americans and Frenchmen, the Belgians rebelled and drove out the Austrians; they wrote a Constitution modeled on our own American Constitution and declared a United States of Belgium. Yet the young republic was too weak to last. Within a few months, its leaders were quarreling among themselves, while the great powers, England, Prussia and, of course, Austria, ordered the new "nation" back to Austria. The United States of Belgium lasted through the year 1790, then dissolved into the Austrian Netherlands. But it did not remain Austrian long. Soon, troops of the French Revolutionary Government, which was at war with Austria, began to swarm in. By 1795, Austria had lost the Southern Netherlands to France.

For the first time since Burgundian days, Liège was included with the other provinces. The Liégeois had bitterly resisted Charles the Bold, but they welcomed French rule, because they admired the ideals so noisily proclaimed by the Revolution and hoped to enjoy the Liberty, Equality and Fraternity which its motto promised. Indeed, in 1789, the example of France had encouraged them to revolt and set up a Republic of Liège, a government which had lasted only a few months longer than the United States of Belgium.

Liège and the other provinces learned almost at once how little happiness or independence French rule brought with it. They were burdened with high taxes and harsh, corrupt French officials. French soldiers looted like enemy troops; citizens were conscripted for service in the French Army. The "defenders" of Liberty, Equality and Fraternity closed, desecrated and even tore down churches, persecuted priests and mocked at all religion. As you might expect, some Belgians protested with a revolt. This time, the uprising came in country districts where peasants armed with scythes, old guns and rusty pikes fought French regular troops. The unequal contest did not last long; the rebels were soon defeated and their leaders executed.

When Napoleon Bonaparte rose to power in France, he corrected certain abuses and restored freedom of worship. Belgium seems to have been the one country outside of France where he was not universally detested; some Belgians admired him; sturdy Flemings and hard-fighting Walloons served in his armies, some even in the Old Guard. Others, however, fought under the British general, Lord Wellington, when in 1815 England, Holland and Prussia finally defeated Napoleon in the Battle of Waterloo, a few miles south of Brussels.

After Waterloo, the victorious allies, having packed Napoleon off to exile on the Island of Saint Helena in the far South Atlantic, began to rearrange the map of Europe, which he had changed to suit himself. They seemed to consider the Southern Netherlands merely as part of the spoils of war and without bothering to consult the wishes of the Southern Netherlanders, or Belgians, joined the territory with Holland in a kingdom called the United Netherlands. In forming a single Netherlands nation, the powers hoped to set up a state large enough and strong enough to block French aggression in the future. They were not concerned about putting together two halves which did not make a whole. They did not stop to consider that, after two centuries and more of separation, the Northern and Southern Netherlands had no love for each other; that memories of religious wars still rankled; that the Protestant Dutch distrusted Catholic Belgians, who returned the feeling. The Southern Netherlands still bore the scars of Dutch invasions, while the silent port of Antwerp loudly accused Holland of strangling Belgian sea trade.

A ruler diplomatic enough to have eased the tensions between

the North and South might in time have united them, but the
new monarch, William I, who had ruled Holland as Prince of
Orange before becoming king of the United Netherlands in 1815,
was neither farseeing nor tactful. Disregarding the fact that Belgium was a Catholic country, he did not hide his contempt for
the religion of his new subjects. He refused to hear Belgian complaints about injustices, real or imagined, and even suppressed
newspapers and punished journalists mentioning the discontent.

Some of the grievances were justified. The Belgians did not
share equally in government with the Dutch as they had been
promised. They were allowed fewer representatives to the Parliament in proportion to their population; almost all cabinet min-
isters, diplomats, army officers and other officials were Dutch.
Since public office in Flanders was now open only to Dutch-speak-
ing applicants, this excluded most upper-class Flemings, whose
education had been French and who spoke, at best, a broken-down
Flemish dialect in addition to French.

As a result, Flanders and Wallonia alike resented William's
severity and grudged Holland its lion's share of authority. Passing
years increased the bad feeling; the Netherlands grew less and
less united until, in 1830, the southern provinces revolted. King
William sent his second son with an army to Brussels to put down
the trouble; his older son refused to fight the Belgians, whom he
was said to prefer to his own Hollanders. After three days of
skirmishing, the Dutch forces withdrew; within three weeks, William had lost the south except for forts at Antwerp and at Maastricht on the Meuse. Eventually, the defenders of Antwerp's
citadel surrendered, but Maastricht was never recovered and has
remained a Dutch city.

The revolutionists proclaimed the independent nation of Belgium. At last, the name Belgium, so often used during the nineteenth century, had become official. From this time on, only
Holland was called the Netherlands. They invited Prince Leopold
of Saxe Coburg to be the first King of the Belgians, a choice Eng-

land approved, since Prince Leopold, though German-born, had been a naturalized British subject. France became a second powerful friend on Leopold's marriage to the daughter of its king. Without the political support of England and actual French military aid against Dutch attempts to retake the territory, it is doubtful whether the nation could have survived the difficult years until Holland was forced to admit that Belgium was on the map to stay.

At last, in 1839, England, France, Prussia, Russia and Austria, meeting in London, recognized a free Belgium, at the same time directing the new nation to remain "perpetually neutral," which meant it must not take sides in any European conflict. Even more, the Treaty of London guaranteed the country against invasion, with each of the five powers promising not only to respect Belgian neutrality but also to defend Belgian territory against any invader.

We might add two postscripts to Belgian-Dutch relations. The first concerns the Scheldt, which had been reopened to traffic as far as Antwerp during the period of the United Netherlands. After the Dutch-Belgian split-up, long negotiations finally brought about agreement to keep the river open. Now Antwerp and Ghent use it freely.

The second postscript has to do with Benelux, a commercial union formed in September 1944 by Belgium, the Netherlands and the Grand Duchy of Luxemburg; the first syllable of each country's name forms the word Benelux. This association has abolished customs duties and nearly all other restrictions on trade across Benelux frontiers. While it does not always work smoothly, the three member countries hope to benefit from the free markets it has created; they also hope the union will draw them into a closer friendship. If the experiment succeeds, not only old Burgundian ambitions but also nineteenth-century aims for a United Netherlands will have come true, in part at least.

7. A COLONY
EIGHTY TIMES AS BIG

KING LEOPOLD I made his entry into Brussels, the capital, on July 21, 1831. The anniversary of that occasion is the country's national holiday. It is celebrated from the polders to the Ardennes with church services, parades, sports contests, carillon concerts, and, in the evening, brilliantly lighted towns, fireworks and dancing in the streets.

Belgium could not have a more suitable national holiday than July 21st, because Leopold's reign began its most peaceful era in ten centuries. The king proved to be wise and tactful at home, a diplomat abroad. While he ruled under a constitution guaranteeing freedom of worship, freedom of education, freedom of the press, this document might not have been fully enforced without him; he made sure that it was properly interpreted and put into effect. Indeed, he used his influence in every way to establish the shaky young nation, with such success that when he died in 1865, Belgium was united and prosperous at home, respected abroad.

His son, Leopold II, did as much for the country, but his contribution was so different, so unusual that it earned him small thanks. Not until after his death did the Belgians realize what they owed him. During his lifetime, his acquisition of the Congo region of Central Africa only irritated and embarrassed his subjects. They could not sympathize with his grandiose ambitions; he for his part was bored by his hard-headed, hard-working people, intent on small, careful profits. He did not relish being king of a little, humdrum state, but dreamed, rather, of ruling an empire, of making millions upon millions of francs to spend as he pleased in building, developing, plunging into money-making schemes or merely indulging his whims. He imagined a Belgium swollen with riches from colonies, perhaps in China, the Philippines, Morocco or along the Nile. Nevertheless, none of his schemes concerning these regions worked out, and he felt frustrated until he began to think of Central Africa.

About that time, the man he needed to help realize his plans, came back to civilization after three years in the heart of Africa. This man was the British-born, naturalized-American journalist, Henry Morton Stanley. You may have heard of the relief party organized by a New York newspaper, which he led into Central Africa to look for the missionary David Livingstone, lost in its wilderness. You have surely heard, too, what Stanley said when, after months of adventure, he found Livingstone deep in cannibal country. His first words were: "Doctor Livingstone, I presume."

Two years after Livingstone's rescue, Stanley undertook another African expedition to trace the course of a river rising in Lake Tanganyika, thinking he might be following the Nile. Three years, thirty cataracts and twenty-five hundred miles later, he reached the mouth of the Congo River. He had fought jungles, heat, disease and the poisoned arrows of cannibal tribesmen; had lost every one of his white companions as well as many of the Arabs from Zanzibar who began the journey with him. Only incredible courage and incredible good luck had brought him out alive from the perils of the largest unexplored area in Africa.

When Stanley returned to Europe with tales of the lands along the river, Leopold persuaded him to enter his service, and sent him back to Africa to extend his explorations, set up trading stations and make treaties with native chiefs by which the king acquired thousands of square miles of Congo territory. In brief, Leopold soon controlled a vast area swelling into Central Africa like a blown-up balloon, with its sole access to the South Atlantic a narrow strip of land along the northern bank of the Congo River.

The king lavished his private fortune on acquiring and developing this realm; he also bullied or wheedled millions of francs from the Belgian government, millions to finance exploration parties, build roads, buy boats—the first steamer to navigate the Congo was a Mississippi River boat. Trading stations sprang up in the African wilds; white men died by the hundreds of heat, disease, snake bite and skirmishes with hostile tribesmen as they supervised the clearing of jungles, the blasting of roads, the erection of shelters and settlements for traders and explorers.

At the same time, thousands of natives died of forced labor and brutal treatment by white and black overseers. The cargoes of natural rubber, the shipments of ivory which began to flow out from the Congo brought with them tales of cruelty that shocked Europe and horrified and embarrassed the Belgians. The government pressed Leopold to let it control the region as he had promised in return for loans made him, but the king clung to his possession, determined that this territory, eighty times the size of Belgium, should remain his private estate so long as he lived, to administer as he chose. Finally, a year before his death, he was forced to cede the colony to Belgium; in 1908, his Congo Free State, which had been anything but free, became the Belgian Congo.

King Albert I, Leopold's nephew, who succeeded him in 1909, helped to establish a new and humane rule for the land. He had been to the Congo, traveling, often on foot, through hundreds and hundreds of miles of forest and jungle; he knew the need for reforms. Not only were reforms made, but thereafter, the colony was governed with thought for the people's well-being. Belgium did not exploit in a selfish way; part of the income from Congo natural resources was invested there in hospitals, schools, sports stadiums; it went to improve agriculture, make roads, build comfortable houses for the natives. Africans, who worked the mines, gathered copra for palm oil, tended coffee, tea, cotton and rubber plants, earned high wages, received good medical care and lived under just laws. Impartial observers called the territory the best-governed, best-fed, best-housed and best-educated between Cairo and Capetown.

Today, the Congo is a bloody, violent, hungry, suffering place. Through the years, the Congolese had no voice in their own government—white men in the country could not vote either—and so the people were not prepared to rule themselves. When they demanded independence, Belgium gave it to them almost immediately and withdrew its officials. The Congolese were not ready for the responsibilities of democracy. As soon as the Republic of Congo was formed in June 1960, it fell apart into violence and chaos. Rival tribes of natives began murdering each other; rival politicians battled each other; white Belgians who had not left the country were often mistreated and sometimes massacred. Troops from the United Nations were sent in almost at once for police duty, but there were times when they could not keep order either.

Of the six Congo provinces, only ore-rich Katanga maintained something like law and decency during this early period. However, Katanga soon seceded from the riotous republic. When it refused to rejoin the so-called central government, United Nations soldiers fought a small war with the Katanga army to force its leaders to yield. Belgians, French and English and some Americans were indignant over the United Nations' treatment of the Katangese. The United Nations' answer to their complaints was that without the mining wealth of Katanga, which is by far the richest part of the Congo, the rest of the country would be bankrupt; that Katanga copper, cobalt, zinc and silver are needed to pay to run any central government.

It is too early to know whether and when the shattered provinces and divided tribes can come together again into a united

Congo. It will take time for the Congo's inhabitants, many of whom are still quite primitive and uneducated, to learn how to live peaceably in a free country. Civil war has undone what fifty years of Belgian efforts tried to accomplish, making the natives almost as miserable now as in the time of King Leopold II.

8. FOUR KINGS
AND TWO WARS

IN 1914, Belgium was stunned by World War I, because after more than eighty years of peace, most Belgians believed the Treaty of London really could guarantee their country's neutrality. Leopold II, less trusting than his people, knew war was possible between France and Germany (in 1871, Prussia had united the other German states into a single nation, with the king of Prussia becoming Emperor of Germany). Fearing such a war might involve Belgium, the king wanted the country ready to repel any invader. Yet he preached preparedness to a nation that seemed hard of hearing. Only with the greatest difficulty did he persuade the government to build forts at Namur and Liège on the Meuse and at Antwerp on the Scheldt. For a long time, too, his plea for universal military training of young men was unpopular; Parliament did not pass a measure providing for it until the king lay dying; he wrote his name for the last time when he signed the bill into law.

Although King Albert, who followed him, also urged the Belgians to arm, they felt too secure under the treaty to think of self-defense. Even when war came between Germany and Austria on one side and France and Russia on the other, most Belgians hoped to remain neutral. They were dumbfounded when the German Minister in Brussels demanded permission for his country's troops to go through Belgium en route to France, promising a peaceful passage if they met no resistance. The king and his government spurned the proposal, telling Germany that Belgium would fight if invaded. Two days later, on August 4, 1914, German troops crossed the frontier and advanced on Liège. The next day, England, under its pledge as a signer of the Treaty of London, declared war on Germany.

King Albert went to the front to command the Belgian Army. He had less than one hundred thousand soldiers; his men lacked sufficient arms and ammunition, but not courage and fighting spirit. The forts at Liège held out for ten days against fierce attacks, time precious to France and England as they made frantic preparations for war. Slowly, fighting steadily, the Belgians retreated across the country to the Yser River in West Flanders. While they held along the Yser in October, King Albert ordered the dikes cut at the place where the Yser flows into the sea near the city of Nieuport. This was done; sea water swirling through the break turned the polders into shallow lakes. The German advance could not continue through the water.

The small patch of Flanders lying between the Yser and the French border and between Nieuport and the city of Ypres was the only part of Belgium the enemy never possessed, although they never gave up trying to take it. After four years of skirmishes, bombings, artillery duels, Ypres lay shattered but still free. Thousands of defenders, many British soldiers among them, had died to keep it so. When peace came again to the city, the people rebuilt their thirteenth-century market hall and their proud cathedral to resemble the old buildings which had been destroyed; yet what draws us to Ypres today are not these restorations of a distant past, but rather memories of our own century, such reminders of the war as the British cemeteries and the handsome Menin Gate. This arch, set into the ruins of the city's medieval ramparts, is inscribed with the words: "Memorial raised in Ypres in honor of the heroism of the British Army and in memory of the fifty-six thousand Tommies who fell in the Ypres salient."

During the war years, from 1914 to 1918, Belgians steadfastly resisted, protested and outwitted the German military occupation. They ceased to be Flemings or Walloons and fused into one people sharing their griefs and hopes for liberation. All kinds of people, encouraged by the example of their leaders, dared to show their patriotism. King Albert with Queen Elizabeth, his wife, remained with the broken army on free Belgian soil, living through the war years in a cottage at La Panne, a fishing village tucked into the dunes. Cardinal Mercier, the head of the Catholic Church in Belgium, defied the Germans time and again, denouncing their injustices. Adolphe Max, the burgomaster of Brussels, defended his people against ever-increasing oppression until he was sent to prison in Germany. German officials complained of Belgian "disobedience." They forgot that these descendants of Southern Netherlanders were merely exercising an old talent for flouting the enemy. Perhaps the Germans had never heard what a French poet said of the country: "Always oppressed but never conquered."

Diaries kept during the occupation contain countless tales of bravery and nearly as many humorous stories. The conquered made fun of their conquerors behind their backs and to their faces; they played sly tricks and had their little jokes on the grimmest days. Sometimes a whole town, hungry and cold, could laugh over how foolish the invaders had been made to seem, as in this story: Pigeon racing is popular in Belgium and pigeon fanciers prize their birds. Therefore, deep resentment met a German order to kill all birds lest they carry military information to the Allies. One man, having obeyed the order, arranged his dead pigeons on the outside window sill of his house under a card on which he had written in large letters: *"Morts pour la Patrie."* This phrase, "Died for the Fatherland" is customarily used in announcing a soldier's death. The German authorities were not amused by his joke and sent him to jail for it—but his townspeople had a good laugh.

When peace came with the defeat of Germany and its allies,

Belgium realized that neutrality on paper was not enough protection, that a modern army would be a better defense than any treaty against aggression in the future. By the fall of 1939, when World War II began, more than six hundred thousand Belgians were under arms. Nevertheless, King Leopold III—his father, Albert, had been killed in 1934 while mountain-climbing in the Ardennes—hoped Belgium could avoid being drawn into the war. During the first eight months while France and Germany merely bristled at each other from their respective lines of forts, Leopold offered to mediate between the enemies. His offers were refused. Then, at dawn on May 10, 1940, without warning, the Nazis attacked neutral Holland, Belgium and Luxemburg. At the same time they invaded France. In four days Holland succumbed to their *Blitzkrieg* or lightning war; French defenses in Northern France quickly crumbled. The Belgian Army held out for eighteen days of horror, but on May 28th, Leopold surrendered.

Though the king was made prisoner, many Belgian officials escaped to England, where they set up a government-in-exile. Thousands of other Belgians slipped out, went to England and joined British fighting forces. Because the Congo continued to export raw materials vital to the Allies, the government in exile could pay Belgium's way in the war. Belgian units with the British infantry, artillery and motorized troops, as well as Belgian aviators flying with the R.A.F. were equipped and maintained with Belgium's own funds.

People who experienced both the first and second German occupations say the second was worse, its hardships greater, the enemy more demanding. Over half a million civilians, women among them, were shipped as slave labor to Germany, many never to return. A typical case was that of the little city of Lierre, near Antwerp. When the Germans occupied the town, they seized eighty men for work in Germany. Of the eighty, forty-two eventually returned; the other thirty-eight had died of overwork and undernourishment.

Through the bad years, plain people and important ones alike behaved with courage. The Rector of Louvain University refused the Nazis a list of his students; he knew they wanted to take from it the names of young men to send off to labor camps. He spent eighteen months in prison for "disobedience." When the Nazis offered the coal miners larger rations than they gave the rest of the country, the miners refused the extra food, saying that what there was should be distributed equally among all Belgians.

The Blitzkrieg destroyed towns that had survived the first war; others were wrecked for the second time in twenty years. In 1914, the Germans had burned the library of Louvain University with its priceless manuscripts and rare books, some printed in the fifteenth century on the earliest presses. Contributions, chiefly from the United States, had rebuilt and restocked the library. In 1940, Nazi bombardment damaged the new building and wiped out the million volumes the university had accumulated between the wars.

Just as Ypres recalls British valor in World War I, so Bastogne symbolizes American heroism in World War II. Because the Allied High Command thought enemy tanks and motorized equipment could not move easily through the thick forests that lay about the town of Bastogne in the Ardennes, they had defended the sector lightly. And for that very reason, the Germans chose to open a surprise offensive here in December 1944, stabbing through the forests to surround the American units stationed in the region. In this Battle of the Bulge, our G.I's were outnumbered by the enemy, encircled, blinded by icy mists and swirling snow. Yet when the Nazis demanded surrender, the American commander, General Anthony McAuliffe, made the now-famous reply, "Nuts." As weather improved and Allied planes could fly in to bomb the enemy, the attack stalled. Soon, American tanks crashed through to the rescue, and within a month the Nazis had withdrawn, the bulge in Allied lines was straightened out, the last serious enemy offensive of the war had failed.

The Nazis retreated from Belgium in the fall of 1944 (except for the December attack in the Ardennes,) leaving too hurriedly to destroy railroads, factories and dock machinery, as they would undoubtedly have done otherwise. No sooner were they gone than the port of Antwerp began handling war supplies, Belgian mills and mines started to produce. Parliament met. As the king was still a prisoner, his brother Prince Charles acted as regent.

When Leopold was released, he came home to hostile subjects. Many resented his unconditional surrender to Germany so early in the war and thought he should have escaped to direct the government-in-exile. Because of the intense feeling against him, the people were asked to vote whether or not they wished him to rule again. Fifty-eight per cent favored his remaining as king, but the minority showed their opposition by such violent strikes and riots that, rather than tear Belgium apart, he abdicated in favor of his son Baudouin, who became king in 1950 at the age of nineteen.

Baudouin is a serious-minded man, although he has become more outgoing since his marriage to a charming Spanish noblewoman. However, his childhood was overshadowed by the death of his mother, a Swedish princess whom the Belgians loved. She died in an automobile accident when Baudouin was four; his father, who was driving at the time of the accident, remained inconsolable for years and Baudouin grew up in a sad home. Belgians say that devotion to his father makes him resent slights which he feels Leopold has suffered. He would not accept the throne until the government agreed to let Leopold live on in Belgium.

Baudouin seems to go earnestly about his job as king, opening a new bridge here, dedicating a pumping station there, visiting a flooded town, laying wreaths on war memorials (usually one for himself and another in his father's name), attending the blessing of carillon bells, giving receptions for newspaper men, chemists, doctors and other visiting delegates to international conventions. He is said to be deeply concerned with social reform, and the laws he has introduced in Parliament are all intended to help his poorer subjects.

As a matter of fact, the king is only one of countless Belgians determined to improve living and working conditions. In recent years, they have accomplished a great deal. For example, fifty years ago the Belgian coal miners were a symbol of misery; today, miners as well as other workers are protected by laws which could scarcely be better.

9. WE BEGIN
TRAVELING

UNTIL NOW we have been going through the past, with a pause here and there for a landmark in Belgian history, but at last the time has come for us to travel across present day Belgium, stopping to see people and places. We can wander through food markets, flower markets, even a rag market where one buys anything from a worn pair of wooden shoes or a second-hand meat cleaver to a battered piano. We may idle away an hour on the wharf of some river town, watching Belgian barges, as well as barges from Holland, Germany, France, tied up or nosing in or out of the stream. We buy fried shrimp at a fried-shrimp stand or a bag of piping hot *frites* (fried potatoes) at a fried-potato stall. Frites are to Belgians what peanuts, popcorn and hot dogs rolled into one are to us. In the museums of a dozen cities, we see paintings, old furniture, lace, arms and armor, ancient manuscripts, Roman coins—all the treasures time has washed down, and which recall the past as seashells echo the sea when held to your ear.

Travel is so easy, interesting towns so near together, that you cannot decide which way to turn, and feel like riding off in all directions at once. For example, if you happen to be in Tournai in the south, you hesitate whether to go on west to Ypres, proceed east to Mons, the prim, pretty city looking down on the grimy coal regions, or swing northeast to Ath for a call on the Giant Goliath and his wife Madame Victory, who live in the town hall.

You would be disappointed in Ath, for the wicker bodies of the giants are taken apart and packed away in sections most of the year. The only time you would be sure to see them is early September when Ath holds its open-air festival and Goliath remarries Madame Victory as part of the fun.

It is even hard to decide whether to enter Belgium from the north, south, east or west. Beyond doubt, the most dramatic approach is by freighter from some United States port direct to Antwerp. Then, as the boat winds up the Scheldt, you see the city rising from land so flat, so netted with canals, so caught in loops of the river that it, too, seems to belong to the sea. This illusion is strongest on a rainy day when the single spire of the cathedral lifting into the low gray sky from the welter of roofs about it, looks as though it has just risen from the ocean where it has been submerged. If you hear the voice of the cathedral's bell, Gabriel, you imagine how its echoes would sound rising from fathoms under water.

Antwerp loses this fairy-tale atmosphere and becomes a lively, worldly place, once you are caught up in its mad traffic, seeing wide boulevards, admiring handsome buildings, old and new, looking into shop windows at lace and leather, cut glass and copper. At night, when neon signs light the downtown sections and trees planted along the main shopping street make weird shadows against the brightness, well-dressed, good-looking people go streaming by, chattering, laughing, greeting friends, drifting in and out of cafes, standing in lines before some movie theater where Frank Sinatra's latest film is showing. You recall the *paseo* or evening promenade in Spain and Spanish-American countries, wondering if you are watching the survival of an old Spanish custom in a Flemish town. Indeed, in almost all the large cities of Belgium, crowds turn out at night, no matter what the weather.

Since Antwerp is so bound to the sea, suppose we explore its water front. If the day is pleasant, we must take a motor launch that pokes into mid-Scheldt and scuds through water traffic to the rhythms of grinding cranes and winches. The thirty miles of Antwerp docks are crowded with ships, for this is one of the world's busiest and most efficient ports.

After the boat ride, we might stroll down the tree-shaded promenade along the docks over which sea-gulls are flying. Now and then we rest on a bench a few feet from some ship being loaded or unloaded, wondering idly as we watch how many days and what oceans lie between it and its home port. Antwerp citizens tell you they are prosperous so long as they have shipping, drydocks where vessels from many lands come for repairs, and diamonds. The city is the world's largest diamond center, with thousands of workers cutting and polishing gray, soapy pebbles into brilliant stones. Diamond cutters came to Antwerp in the sixteenth century and have been here ever since except during World War II. Then those who could escape fled the country before the Nazis took over. The rest were sent to concentration camps. You see, most of the diamond cutters are Jews.

If we still feel in a sea mood, the Steen, looming above the wharf where we boarded the launch, houses an interesting collection of ship models and other maritime exhibits. Centuries ago, the Steen was a fortress; later, it became a prison; now, old and crumbling, it is a museum, and next-door neighbor to the United States Lines. Perhaps as you climb the ramp leading to its medieval courtyard you see the smokestack of some American vessel, say *The Keystone State,* poking above the fortifications like an ancient war machine.

In the narrow streets twisting away from the docks, you pass seamen from every ocean, are intrigued by voices speaking many languages, by raucous laughter and cheap music coming from taverns in the tall houses. This sailor must be just home from Brazil or some other southern port, for he carries a parrot in a cage as he swings along; those swarthy men in red fezzes and rumpled European clothes are Arabs. What a background, what types for a mystery story or adventure movie are all about you! You peer into shop windows at rope, wooden shoes, oilskins, pea jackets, rosaries, flashlights, tubes of American shaving cream and packages of American chewing gum. Here and there above you, a statue of the Virgin smiles down from a niche in a corner house.

Follow the winding streets a little farther and you may come into a large square, the Green Square beside the cathedral or the Grand' Place, where ancient guild houses look over at the fine town hall. Inside the town hall, one splendid room opens into another, wood-paneled, tapestried, decorated with mural paintings. You may visit the burgomaster's office, the city council chamber, the marriage hall where the burgomaster or one of his deputies performs the civil marriage required of every couple in Belgium; usually this is followed by a church wedding. One of the beautiful rooms displays a tablet presented to Antwerp by President Eisenhower when he was the Supreme Allied Commander, commending the people of Antwerp for their courage during seven months of German rocket bomb attacks. After the city was reoccupied by the Allies, from October 13, 1944 to May 29, 1945, rockets destroyed twenty thousand homes and killed three thousand citizens of Antwerp.

A bomb exploding in the Friday Market before the Plantin Museum, shattered its windows, cracked its walls and ripped open the roof. However, the contents of the house had been carefully stored away beforehand and so careful repairs after the war restored this record of Antwerp life. The enormous house was the home and shop of the Plantin-Moretus family, whose presses, as you recall, once turned out the handsomest books in the Netherlands.

Christopher Plantin, the founder of the business, bought a house on this site in 1579 from a Spanish merchant, calling it the Golden Compasses; later, adjoining houses were added to the first building. Here, with the help of scholars from Louvain and other universities of Europe, Plantin undertook to publish the Polyglot Bible, so called because on its pages the Latin, Greek, Hebrew,

Syrian and Chaldaic texts of the Bible appeared in parallel columns. The project delighted King Philip II of Spain but almost
beggared Plantin because Philip was too miserly to reimburse
him for what the work cost.

After Plantin's death, his son-in-law Jan Moretus maintained
the high standards of craftsmanship and learning, but the Moretus
descendants gradually lost the firm's reputation for fine work.
However, out of respect for tradition, they preserved every possible shred of the past with such care that when in 1876, a Moretus
closed out the business and sold the house to the city of Antwerp,
it could be opened to the public as a rich museum of other days,
the home of a family of culture and riches, as well as the only museum of printing in the world.

Everything in this enormous stone and brick mansion is so complete, so authentic you are sure the owner and his staff have only
just left it for the day; this summer morning they may be out
watching the *Ommegang*, a traditional parade (which is still held)
pass through the streets. So, while typesetters, copyreaders, ap-
prentices and the master himself are away, you look at their
presses—still used on special occasions—their cases of type, the
foundries with molds, anvil, grindstone and smelting furnace. You
pause in the small dark shop with barred windows and a door
opening into Holy Ghost Street. On the long counter stand scales
which merchants of the past used for weighing silver and gold
coins given them, to be sure they were the proper weight. You
look at portraits of the Plantin and Moretus family on the walls;
eighteen were painted by Rubens. In other rooms, the walls are
hung with tapestries or covered with leather embossed in intri-
cate designs and gilded.

In a case exhibiting rare books published by the firm you spot
a colored sketch said to be the first made of the potato plant and
the potato after it was brought to the Old World. Finally, you
stare through leaded windows into the courtyard where moss
turns the cobbles green, and admire the vine clinging to the old

brick walls. Your guide book says Christopher Plantin himself is thought to have planted the vine.

Rubens' house does not evoke its master so vividly as the Plantin Museum. This may be because the building is a reconstruction of the mansion the painter built for himself, a skillful reconstruction, but not the original. Nevertheless, it is a charming spot. The garden is enchanting with its flower beds and long arbor, and you cannot stand in the balcony above the artist's great, two-story high studio without peopling it with his students working at their easels as he walks among them, suggesting and criticizing. A door to the right of the balcony reaches to the ceiling; it was built this way so that enormous paintings could be moved out easily when finished.

Probably Rubens' masterpiece, *The Descent from the Cross,* went through the tall door. Now, with a companion painting, *The Elevation of the Cross,* it flanks the main altar of the cathedral of Antwerp, while over the altar is a third great Rubens' picture, *The Assumption of the Virgin,* which shows Christ's mother reclining on a cloud as she floats to heaven surrounded by adoring cherubs.

There is much more to see and do in Antwerp: you can go to its zoo in the center of town, one of the best in Europe; you can visit old churches, stroll through open air markets or buy souvenirs in fine shops, spend hours in the art museum which contains a splendid collection of Flemish paintings, visit several smaller collections shown in what were once private houses. Antwerp is hard to leave. Once you have decided to do so, you face the problem so usual in Belgium: By which road?

Shall you go southwest through farmlands where North Sea winds drive the windmills and blow in the salt spray? Fifteen miles in that direction is Saint Nicholas, the town with the largest public square in Europe—seven acres of it. That, however, is not why Saint Nicholas deserves a visit. Even its picturesque old buildings do not draw you as does the museum in which two large rooms are dedicated to Gerard Mercator, the sixteenth century geographer and scholar. You may have puzzled at the Mercator map of the world which makes North America look so much larger than South America because all the meridians are drawn parallel. Mercator was born near Saint Nicholas, but you learn to know him best here in the museum among the maps he drew, copies of books he wrote and two globes he made, one of crystal showing the heavens and the other, a wooden globe representing the earth.

Instead of taking the trip to Saint Nicholas, shall you go on to Brussels? If so, a short detour from the Brussels road brings you to Lierre. Try to see Lierre on a sunny morning, a sunny Sunday morning. Then you will never forget its spires and treetops outlined against the pale northern sky, its turreted belfry beside the city hall and the thin River Nethe coiling through the fields around the town. Gabled houses look through shining windows at clean, narrow streets where people hurry to and from church, sturdy, rosy men and women, and children polished with soap and water. Nowhere are there such scrubbed young faces and knees as in Belgium.

In the Beguinage behind the high wall shutting it away from the city all about, flags flap against the red and white brick house fronts. Some are Belgian flags; on others, you recognize the black lion of Flanders. Women are out scrubbing their doorsills and sprinkling the street with bright confetti. In the Beguinage church, the children are making their solemn communion. When the service is over, they will march down the flag-hung lanes of the Beguinage, over cobbles and confetti, carrying gay banners and singing.

Poor families live in the Beguinage now, because the Beguines are gone. In 1956 only one old Beguine remained of all those who have worked and prayed in the tiny houses down through the centuries. The word Beguinage may be new to you because, with the exception of two in Holland, this has been purely a Belgian institution. The eight-hundred year old order of Beguines resembles in many ways an order of nuns. However, a Beguine, unlike a nun, does not take permanent religious vows and so is free to go back into the world and resume her former life whenever she wishes. In the Middle Ages, rich and noble ladies often entered a Beguinage to lead a life of prayer and piety, bringing their fortunes to help the community, but such prosperity ended long ago and the Beguinages have been poor for a long time. Beguines must earn their living by sewing and mending, doing embroidery, making lace and going out as nurses. Today, no young girls are joining the order and the old sisters are gradually dying; many Beguinages have lost their last Beguine, for example those at Malines and Bruges. In a few, three or four very old sisters remain among the people who have occupied the houses of the little settlement. Children play in the cobbled streets and grassy squares of the city within a city, and only rarely do you see a woman in the Beguine's habit of white Flemish headdress and full black gown moving among them.

Buyers for American stores go to Lierre for beaded bags; Lierre women also make lace, and the town manufactures brass musical instruments. However, at mention of Lierre, most people think of the Zimmer Tower, a seventeenth-century structure renamed in 1930 for Louis Zimmer, a local watchmaker and astronomer. In that year, Zimmer installed in the tower an elaborate system of dials controlled by a clock mechanism. The clock, encircled by twelve other dials covers the upper third of one face of the tower. The dials give you all kinds of information. One indicates the day of the week, another, the day of the month; a third lets you compute the day of the week on which every date falls within a cycle of twenty-eight years. The prettiest dial shows the phases of the moon by means of a globe which turns its blue-painted side at the dark of the moon and, as the moon waxes, grows from a golden sliver to a full gold face, then dwindles with the waning moon.

In a second-floor room of the tower, fifty-seven other dials cover the walls with fascinating facts, such as what time it is at the moment in Holland, say, and France; in Turkey, the Philippines, New York, San Francisco. You find out about the movement of the tides in Lisbon, Ostend, Iceland, Saigon among other places; about the revolution of the planets around the sun, and eclipses of the sun and moon. One dial shows the hour according to a decimal clock. This system divides the day and night into ten hours altogether, each hour being one hundred forty-four minutes long. Thus five o'clock corresponds to noon, while ten o'clock is midnight. This clock was used during the French Revolution, but the guide who shows it to you, predicts that, while it was the time of the past, it will surely be the time of the future also.

10. MALINES
AND LOUVAIN

ABOUT eight miles south of Lierre on the road to
Brussels, lies Malines or Mechelen, if you prefer its Flemish name.
Malines is famous, among other things, for medieval buildings,
carillon music and vegetables. Big American trucks and an occasional bright blue, horse-drawn wagon haul in to the city markets
the big, sweet strawberries, cauliflowers, white asparagus and chicory, which is called endive outside Belgium and looks like a long,
pale flower bud; it is so white because it has been grown in the
dark. If we use endive at all in the United States, we put it into
a salad, but Europeans prepare it as a delicious hot vegetable.

Not so long ago, the produce brought into Malines was shipped
out on barges from quays along the River Dyle. Now the crates
and baskets are trucked to all parts of the country, while the
wharves and the river lie idle except for an occasional barge bringing other merchandise and, in fall, winter and spring, the fishing
boats which put in with their catch of mussels.

But the Dyle still smells brackish, the North Sea winds scour
the houses that have fronted on the river for centuries, and tides
come up just as when Malines was a busy port. Four hundred
years ago, the city was also the capital of the Netherlands. That
was while Margaret of Austria acted as regent for her nephew,
Charles V. The palace where she brought up young Charles and
his sisters after their father died and they could no longer live

with their insane mother, is now the court house, a fascinating building with a steep roof full of small, gabled windows which overlook the grass and flowers of the courtyard. Margaret was the daughter of Maximilian and Mary of Burgundy, and a true Burgundian in her interest in art and learning, her love of beautiful things. Musicians, scholars and artists came to her court; she kept the artists busy carving, chiseling, painting and building.

Saint Rombaut's Cathedral in Malines, begun a century before her time, was finished during her life. It looms above the gables and high-walled gardens of Malines and its tower, taller than a twenty-story building, rises in dark grandeur. Its voice is the sweetest in Belgium.

Lovers of music know Saint Rombaut's carillon, and they have heard about Jef Denyn, the carillonneur, who perfected and enriched bell music, whose concerts at Saint Rombaut's brought visitors to Malines from everywhere. In 1922, Denyn founded the only carillon school in existence. He taught many musicians now in the United States, while today others are studying under his successor. In 1953, the school dedicated its own carillon in a slim, red-brick tower which looks as though it belongs in the background of a van der Weyden painting.

If you climb up to see the forty-nine bells of Saint Rombaut or those in the school belfry, you look over row upon row of bells, hung tier above tier, the largest fitted into heavy wooden framework below the lighter bells, which hang from upper frames according to their diminishing size and weight. The biggest bells stand taller than a man and weigh eight tons or more; the smallest are from ten to twelve inches high and a mere twenty pounds light.

You may recall how, in early Netherlands history, bells warned of storm, fire and invaders. Not until the fourteenth century, however, did their voices blend into music. Then mechanical clocks installed in church towers and town belfries could move the bells to make them toll the hour, the half hour and the quarter hour. As soon as it was found that the clock mechanism operated the bells, more and more were added until their range of tones were fused into tunes, usually played just before the clock struck. Thus, the carillon became a musical instrument. Later, the invention of a keyboard enabled a musician to play the carillon somewhat as he would a pipe organ, with the small bells moved by hand controls and the heavy ones by foot pedals.

At one time Belgium had more than a hundred singing towers. Today about sixty carillons remain in town halls and church towers, comprising anywhere from twenty-five to fifty-odd bells. In summer, cities like Malines, Ghent and Bruges schedule regular keyboard concerts, but usually in most towns you hear the mechanical music produced by perforated cylinders which look like the rolls of a giant old-fashioned music box and turn as they play. Pins set into the perforations form a musical pattern which determines the tunes for the folk songs, hymns and patriotic airs played by the clock mechanism. Some may surprise you, as in Malines when Saint Rombaut's carillon peals out "Hail, hail, the gang's all here" just before the clock strikes the hour.

To be thrilled by a carillon, you must hear a keyboard concert by a good musician, because then the belfry seems to speak for the sky. High notes eddy far above, light as raindrops, deeper tones spatter in gusts of silver, and the heavy bells chant like gales at sea. Melodies swirl, scatter, throb and swell, suffusing the air and drenching you with music.

Once a city of lacemakers, Malines has all but lost the art. So-called Malines lace now comes from Tournhout, a city to the northeast near the Dutch border. Only occasionally on a fine day do you see a woman sitting outside her door with a pillow before her, weaving the threads from countless bobbins through a maze of pins which prick out the lace design on a pattern spread out on the pillow. If you could watch her work through days and weeks, you would see these twisting threads fill in birds, butterflies, flowers and figures in a delicate mesh.

Lacemaking has been taught in Belgium for centuries, especially in convents and Beguinages, but every year fewer girls and women come to learn the art. It is dying, because lace brings the maker too little and costs the buyer too much. For instance, a woman spends two months working on enough of a filmy edging called fairy lace to put around a tiny linen square of handkerchief; the handkerchief sells for twenty dollars! As most of the lacemakers now are elderly, the time will surely come when they no longer work and sing together as they have done for centuries, their hands moving to the rhythms of ancient religious songs, love songs and ballads about knights and knightly deeds.

Nevertheless, if you can afford handmade lace, you still may buy all you want in Belgium—scarves, handkerchiefs, doilies, table mats and covers, lace fans, wedding veils. Some of these laces are made with a needle and a single thread; others grow under the weaving bobbins. The type varies also with the locality where it is made: Bruges lace differs from that made in Binche; Malines is not the same as Brussels lace, which, by the way, is almost always the choice for bridal veils.

The trip from Malines to Brussels takes fifteen minutes by clean, comfortable, frequent trains. Brussels, at the center of Belgium's transportation net, draws the rest of the country to it like a magnet; you commute to Ghent, Louvain or Antwerp with the same ease as you go out from New York to surrounding suburbs. Service to eastern and southern Belgium is also good; only North Sea towns near the French and Dutch borders and points in the far Ardennes are too remote for a round trip in one day.

One of the best ways to see Belgium is to settle down in Brussels and go out from it to places that interest you. Each one-day excursion tempts you to another. No matter where you go, the country is lovely—if you can overlook the blotches made by mining and factory districts in a few sections. The more you travel, the more you notice how the landscape to the north and west differs from that to the east and south. Toward Ghent and Bruges, the coastal plain is broken by lines of willows and locusts, by clumps of chestnut trees and pines; it is divided into narrow fields, every inch under cultivation, and dotted with low, red-roofed farmhouses, some of red brick, others white with bright blue shutters and doors, yellow with blue trim, or even blue—very blue, against green shutters and doors.

From Brussels east to Louvain, the land swells gently as though already lifting towards the Ardennes. Village after village crowds the horizon with dark roofs, above which rises an occasional square brick tower, but more often a slate steeple shaped like a bell, a top or a thin dunce cap. Apple, peach and cherry orchards shelter behind rows of thickly-planted poplars and the fields are wider, with now and then some land lying fallow. Here a farmer is driving a tractor; there, one of the powerful Brabant horses is at work. These animals with smoothly rounded body and butterscotch-colored coat trimmed in long creamy tail and mane are as beautiful as pottery figures.

The trip to Louvain is worth making. You think the city's fifteenth-century town hall should be carved in ivory instead of stone and shrunk to jewel-case size—it is so delicate and elaborate. You find a melancholy charm in the white and yellow houses of the Beguinage where one of the four remaining Beguines shows you through the Beguinage church, which like the town hall has escaped the ruin that centuries of wars have brought. The city has been so lovingly repaired and rebuilt on old plans that you still see it as a medieval town of turrets, spires, gables and streets following the meanders of the Dyle.

You visit the university library and feel welcome there, almost at home, for the library is a symbol of Belgian-American friendship. You may recall how, after World War I, the people of the United States contributed most of the money needed to construct a new library replacing the one burned by the Germans. An American architect designed the present building with its steep Flemish roof and marble façade lighted by long, leaded windows.

As you come into the deep, covered entrance, you notice that every pillar is carved in gold letters with the name of some group which gave to the building fund: Almost all the names are of American associations. You read: "Public Schools of New York City," "Parochial Schools of New York City," "Johns Hopkins University," "The University of Texas," "Friends Central School" (of Philadelphia) and many others.

The bombing of Louvain in World War II burned the library's books but did not damage the building beyond repair. Nor did it harm the tower rising from an inner courtyard. Here hang fifty-eight bells of a carillon given by the engineers of the United States. The enemy took down many bells during World War II and shipped them off to Germany, but Louvain's carillon escaped this fate; its giant bell hangs undisturbed in the tower with this inscription on it:

> "The Liberty Bell of Louvain: This Carillon in Memory of the Engineers of the United States of America, who gave their Lives in the Service of their Country and her Allies in the Great War of 1914-1918."

When you look at the tower from the square before the library, you notice that it has a clock dial high up which shows twelve stars instead of numbers to mark the hours. Each side of the tower has such a dial, thus making forty-eight stars in all, or one for each state in our union.

The library is the one building which the seven thousand students of Louvain University share in common, for the university has no campus and its colleges and lecture halls are scattered through the city. Only in the library do law students, those studying fine arts, archeology and other advanced subjects have a common meeting place. You see them at work in the long, paneled reading room or talking quietly in the halls. In the town, you meet them bicycling to class, strolling through the crooked streets; you see them, too, sitting over beer or coffee, talking, playing cards or chess, in some cafe near the Grand' Place in the shadow of the town hall. Now and then you hear of a student prank, but usually these young men—and girls too—are serious and well behaved.

Perhaps they feel they must maintain the prestige of their university. Louvain is one of the old schools of Europe, younger to be sure than the University of Paris or Oxford or Salamanca in Spain, but equally famous in the later Middle Ages. A fifteenth-century pope was one of its alumni; in the next century, the Emperor Charles V studied there, as well as scholars like Erasmus, the learned Hollander, who founded one of the university colleges, Sir Thomas More, the Englishman, whose *Utopia*, or plan for an ideal state, was first published in Louvain, and Mercator, the geographer.

Louvain is the Catholic University of Belgium; Ghent and Liège were established early in the last century as government universities, while the free University of Brussels is controlled by that city. Louvain and Brussels teach courses in both French and Flemish. In 1955, Ghent had a great celebration of its twenty-fifth anniversary as a Flemish school, with King Baudouin and many scholars and government officials attending the ceremonies. However, for many years after its foundation in 1816 Ghent had been a French-language institution deep in the heart of Flanders, and faculty and students alike, although many were Flemish born, opposed early Flamingant demands that it teach in Flemish. During World War I, the Germans ordered this change made in the hope of earning Flamingant gratitude and support, but they misjudged the Belgians. Most Flamingants resented such interference. Flamingant leaders wrote the German authorities: "We are of a race which has always managed its own affairs on its own soil." After 1918, Ghent resumed the use of French and it was not until 1930 that the change-over was made to Flemish.

Belgian universities are coeducational. They are professional or graduate schools, and young women who want to be doctors or

lawyers or do advanced work in any field attend on an equal foot-
ing with the men.

However, below university level, boys and girls are in separate
schools from the time they enter the primary grades at the age of
six until they finish high school twelve years later. The *athénée*
is the boys' high school; girls go to a *lycée*. If the town is too small
to afford two high schools, then girls are admitted to the athénée
with the boys.

Belgian boys and girls work harder in school than American
children; they have little or no class time for exercises and sports,
and yet their school life cannot be too dull because many field
trips vary the routine. You meet them everywhere, marching two
by two in long files, the girls in thin cotton dresses, the boys wearing the shortest of shorts on the coolest, rainiest day. You see
them, never straggling or misbehaving, examining pictures in the
art galleries of Antwerp and Brussels, climbing the mound at
Waterloo for a visit with the lion on top and a view across the battlefield, looking at Congo exhibits in the Museum at Tervueren,
in Saint Bavon's Cathedral listening to a lecture on the van Eyck
painting of the *Adoration of the Mystic Lamb;* you are almost
swept off the street by a column of older boys, accompanied by a
priest, rushing into a public bathhouse.

11. GHENT, THE CITY
OF CONTRASTS

AFTER BRUSSELS, foreigners usually know Ghent and Bruges better than other Belgian towns. Both deserve to be visited again and again, for they are rich art cities, evoking memories of a splendid and tempestuous past. Ghent has stood for more than a thousand years where the rivers Lieve and Lys join the Scheldt. It is a water town on a maze of eighty islands linked by two hundred bridges and yet it prefers to be called "the city of flowers." As suitable a name would be "city of contrasts," because contrasts are everywhere: in gray stone and dark brick surrounded by flowers, in old buildings and new ideas; in signs of hard-headed practicality combined with elegance and love of beauty. No city in Belgium has had such haughty aristocrats; nowhere in Belgium is socialism more of a force. The statue honoring the weavers of Ghent is pointed out to tourists; so, too, are the fine old mansions, some still privately owned, which are veritable museums of paintings and antiques. Ghent is both an art city and a key industrial center. Men become rich here in the linen- and cotton-weaving business; they also prosper growing orchids under acres of glass, and azaleas and begonias that bloom in fields to the east and west of town.

Ghent still has several fortresses, but the one built by England after the Battle of Waterloo was torn down to make the Citadel Park. This is a place of lawns and shining pools, fragrant in May

with lilacs and shaded by red-flowering hawthorn trees; it is known
for its rose garden and the garden of Alpine plants near the Flo-
ralia Palace. Every five years, an international flower show in this
palace brings more than a million visitors to Ghent in one week.

The city's most famous fortress is the Castle of the Counts of
Flanders, reflected in the dark waters of the Lieve. This citadel,
modeled after a crusader's castle in the Holy Land, has seen Ghent
battle through eight centuries. Sentries on its donjon tower
watched men march out to join the workers of Bruges in the victory of the Golden Spurs; other sentries, peering through slits in
the battlements must have witnessed the bloodiest of many bloody
guild struggles, when a thousand weavers and fullers died at each
others' hands. King Edward III of England banqueted in one of
its gloomy halls with Jacques van Artevelde. Here, while fiddlers
played on and on, Duke Philip the Good of Burgundy drank from
golden goblets with knights of the Golden Fleece and feasted at
a table covered with black velvet embroidered in the arms of Burgundy. Charles V frequently came here; in the castle courtyard,
twenty leaders of the rebellion against him were executed. The
ghosts of countless other prisoners must haunt the dungeons and
torture chambers.

The past lies all about the Castle of the Counts. Not far away,
in the paneled hall of the Sint Jorishof (Saint George's Court),
Mary of Burgundy signed a charter of liberty for Flanders; the
lion in the mantel above the vast fireplace was carved, they say,
to commemorate the event. You may have lunch at a table near
the fireplace, for the Sint Jorishof is a hotel, and has been one for
seven hundred years. If you prefer, you may sit in a second dining
room with leaded windows looking out on the street and the town
hall across the way; perhaps as you sit dreaming of princes, knights
and burghers, a big red trailer truck loaded with newsprint rum-
bles past on its way from the port, as if to shake you back into the
twentieth century. This second dining room, like the first, is decorated with plates, mugs and other trophies for crossbow marks-

manship, all won by members of the family which has owned the hotel for generations. The present proprietor has been the crossbow champion of Europe for many years, and his title is very suitable, since the Guild of Saint George, the crossbowmen, established headquarters in this building five centuries ago.

The belfry is just down the square from the Sint Jorishof. Guide books usually mention the eleven-foot-high brass dragon on the spire, some claiming it was brought from Constantinople, others admitting it is as Flemish as the sturdy belfry. Nevertheless, not one reveals that Dragon the First, which went aloft in 1377, abdicated a hundred years ago to a glittering new counterpart. If you take the elevator which limps up through the tower, you may get off at the floor where the original dragon, worn to a black metal skeleton by the winds of East Flanders, reposes with other mementos such as ancient bells, models of the belfry at different stages of its history, even one of Napoleon Bonaparte's big hats in a glass case. At another level of the belfry the great bell Roland hangs with several companions near its own size. On a third story is the metal cylinder on which the carillon tunes are played mechanically. Near it stands the keyboard the carillonneur plays when he gives special concerts—such a small keyboard to move Roland and other big bells, as well as the smaller ones hung in the room at the top of the tower! No American should hear the carillon at Ghent without recalling that on Christmas Eve, 1814, its music announced the signing of the Treaty of Ghent, which meant that the United States and England had made peace after the War of 1812.

Ghent has built a port connected by a twenty-mile-long canal north to a point in Holland near the mouth of the Scheldt; its water traffic is next greatest to that of Antwerp. After you have gone out to see the tankers and ocean-going freighters at the modern docks, you may want to come back and wander along the *Graslei,* or Grass Quay, where water trade goes on in the ancient way, with barges and small craft loading or unloading sacks, boxes,

bales, barrels from the cobbled wharves at the foot of the beautiful old warehouses and guild houses with their elaborate gables
and gilding.

Even the small Beguinage huddled behind a high white wall
feels the present in spite of its sleepy, medieval-village look. Sixty
elderly Beguines occupy the tiny houses of red brick trimmed
with white stone, each bearing its name on a brass plaque: *Huis*
(house) of Our Lady of Lourdes, of Saint Modestus, of Saint
Eleanor, etc. The Beguines worship in their elaborate church
and wear age-old, traditional costumes, but they cannot hold off
passing time. Their number is decreasing and they realize that
the order will disappear with them. For a moment, you may have
the illusion that nothing has changed in the quiet settlement, but
as you stand near the entrance gate talking with an old sister, a
delivery boy goes by wheeling a hand truck through the gate.
There are three cases of empty Coca Cola bottles on the truck!

Ghent deserves to be visited day after day, to be described on
page after page, because it offers so much. You must see the Rabot,
a small gray fortress with pointed slate towers on the River Lieve,
and that other citadel known as the Castle of Gerard the Devil,
which was built as a nobleman's stronghold in the Middle Ages.
The Botanic Gardens contain plants from everywhere, notably
the Victoria Regia, a great, rose-colored water lily from the Ama-
zon. You must go into Saint Bavon's Cathedral planted on thou-
sand-year old foundations, stark and dark outside but crowded
and rich within, cluttered with black and white marble, paintings,
carved wood, gold and silver vessels, gleaming bronze. In a side
chapel, the panels of the *Adoration of the Mystic Lamb* glow as
brightly as though the brothers van Eyck had only just laid down
their brushes and paints.

When we think of men who helped make the history of Ghent,
the Netherlands and Europe, we recall Jacques van Artevelde and
Charles V. Of course, many others have been as important, but
we have not taken the time to know them. However, before leav-

ing the city, we must meet a third native son who had nothing to do with his birthplace after he left it, and yet of whom Ghent is now very proud. This man is Maurice Maeterlinck, the poet and dramatist, who belongs to our own century—he died in 1949. Maeterlinck was born in Ghent of well-to-do parents and educated there, but not until he became famous abroad, did the city regret its mockery of his early writing and acknowledge his genius. By then he had left Belgium to spend the rest of his life in France, returning only on business or for family reasons.

Since Maeterlinck wrote his dreamy, whimsical plays in French, he is often thought of as a French author. Yet he remains as Flemish as Ghent itself. Look at his photograph: his lips are full, his face is broad, strong, quiet. Read the careful, precise instructions he gives for stage sets and costumes in his plays; they suggest the careful details painted by a Flemish master. Read a few pages of *Pelleas and Melisande,* the haunting tragedy which charmed the composer Claude Debussy into using it as the libretto for an opera by that name. Read *The Blue Bird,* a fantasy that has given us the symbol for happiness. The imagination in these plays are as Belgian as dragon weathervanes, as fanciful as the grotesque giants which many towns parade through their streets; in them, the sense of the supernatural resembles Belgian regard for the saints and Belgian religious feeling.

12. BRUGES,
THE DREAMER

THE POET who first spoke of "Bruges, the Dead" invented an expression that should have worn out long ago from overwork. Almost every tourist knows the term; guide books are sure to use it. Although the words cast a melancholy spell, they do not describe the drowsy, lovely ancient city or its citizens. Bruges may seem to sleep, to dream, but it is not dead, merely breathing slowly; in the summer, unfortunately, it is breathing the foul odor of sluggish canals.

Old ways of life survive in the narrow, cobbled streets, in canals where swans drift and trees sketch leaf patterns on dark walls beside the water, in the tiny, cream-colored row houses, each capped by a miniature gable, which were built centuries ago to shelter the city's poor, in the Beguinage beside the Lake of Love, where willow trees weep into the water all summer though. There are no Beguines left, but nuns occupy the ivory and rose-red houses around the square where grass is high under the trees; they make lace and embroidery to sell to tourists and for a few francs take you through a Beguine's dwelling as it was in the old days. It consists of four small rooms enclosing a courtyard, and is furnished with porcelain stove, heavy oak furniture and blue earthenware dishes.

Although Bruges is not a large city, it is a very tiring one. As you walk about, there is always something else to see just around the corner! You pause at every other step to examine a crumbling coat of arms over a door, a saint's statue in a niche, a weathervane, a balcony swung over the water, a garden guessed at behind high walls. Each quay, each bridge over a canal opens vistas of turrets, towers and gardens, a view of gables designed in rickrack or scallops against the sky.

The belfry seems to be everywhere, so simple and yet so graceful as it stems from the medieval cloth hall where in the days of Bruges' greatness, woolen merchants bargained and feasted, perhaps with traders from Russia and bankers from Italy. The belfry dwarfs the cloth hall and looms too large over the square. Yet what a thrilling tower it is, as it thrusts up from foundations laid on thousands of stakes driven into the marshy ground. If you climb four hundred steps to its top, on a fine day you see across spires and greenery, rusty red roofs and gleaming ribbons of water to the polders melting into a mist that is the North Sea.

The Chapel of Saint Basil in the shadow of the belfry is really two chapels, a dark, low-vaulted ground-floor and an upper one, gilded and painted. People usually speak of Saint Basil's as the Chapel of the Holy Blood, because the upper chapel was built to hold the vessel said to contain drops of blood which Christ shed while He was on the cross. Thierry of Alsace, Count of Flanders brought the relic home from the Second Crusade and presented it to the city. The citizens of Bruges consider it their greatest treasure. Once a week, crowds kneel in the upper chapel as the relic is displayed. Once a year, on the first Monday after May second, the gold casket containing the relic, accompanied by the clergy, church societies and the aristocracy of the city, is carried with ancient pageantry to the cathedral and then brought back to Saint Basil's.

The Hospital of Saint John, where you see Hans Memling's masterpieces, is at some distance from the Chapel of the Holy Blood and the belfry, but it is near the Church of Notre Dame. In a small bare chapel of Notre Dame, gilded copper effigies of Mary of Burgundy and her father, Charles the Bold, lie on tombs side by side. Charles wears armor; his helmet and gauntlets are beside him; his feet rest on a crouching lion. Mary's two little dogs are at her feet, her many coats of arms in brilliant enamels cover the sides of the tomb. She looks young and royal in an embroidered mantle and tight cap beneath the crown set back from her high forehead; her hands are folded in prayer; she seems a golden figure Memling might have painted in blue and rose and cream.

Bruges may be very old, but its houses are kept in repair, the city is spotless and flowers bloom on the quays and even in baskets about the lamp posts; the carillon spatters bars of music before the clock strikes—on a sunny day, the city is gay as a fairy story. The people you meet look healthy and cheerful. Women sitting in the street outside their doors making lace by old patterns are gay and friendly as they offer you their work for sale; fishermen from Zeebrugge, the port of Bruges, have a lively time in the open-air fish market as they sell their catch to Bruges housewives; merchants hang banners with fanciful guild emblems over their doors to announce a *braderie* or bargain day; schoolboys, priests, workmen, shoppers, clerks steer coveys of bicycles through the narrow streets past tourist buses and trucks big enough to flatten them against a house front, and seem to enjoy their brush with traffic.

You admire the Belgian talent for keeping the past alive when you visit a certain dark red, fifteenth century palace on the outskirts of Bruges, with its finger-thin tower lifted in the shadow of the last two windmills near the town. This is the house of the Guild of Saint Sebastian, the longbowmen. In the past, the longbowmen were a powerful guild; now Saint Sebastian's in Bruges is an exclusive club. Its members claim the guild was already formed when longbowmen went off from Bruges and other cities of the Netherlands to the First Crusade at the end of the eleventh century. However, some historians say that the archers with the longbow did not organize until two hundred years later, just after the Battle of the Golden Spurs. Of course, the longbow was used centuries before then. The question of dates seems important because the rival guild, the crossbowmen of Saint George, insist that their order was established in 1213, nearly a hundred years before the Battle of the Golden Spurs. No wonder Saint Sebastian's men are anxious to fix an earlier date for their foundation!

Both groups were powerful in the Middle Ages, since a corps of skilled bowmen might decide a battle. Rulers sought the good will of the hard-headed, independent archers of the Netherlands, whose help they often needed. In Ghent, Brussels and other cities besides Bruges, counts and dukes competed with weavers, gardeners, brewers and bankers for championship honors; a king was proud to win the title of *Roi du Tir* or King of the Range. In Brussels, Charles V, who loved all sports, shot down the wooden bird set up as a target—on a church spire, it is said. This feat gave him the right to be king of the archers as well as King of Spain.

When the use of gunpowder made bows and arrows old-fashioned, the Belgians, loyal as always to their traditions, changed archery from a war game to a sport and they have kept on practicing their shots ever since.

Today in Bruges, behind the palace, the gentlemen of Saint Sebastian shoot with sharp-tipped aluminum arrows at a target at the end of a long alley of clipped trees, or else they go out into the meadow beyond the alley hedge to shoot blunt, wooden arrows from the protection of a roofed-over stand at wooden birds swinging on a hundred-foot-high pole. The boys who retrieve the arrows and birds wear heavy hats made of braided willow with a brim wide enough to protect their shoulders from falling objects. An ash tree, planted at the right place, shades the archers' eyes during the hours when competitions are held: a contest invariably begins at five o'clock in the afternoon.

The best shot wins the title of king of the guild, and in Bruges he keeps the honor for life, although other archery clubs make the champion defend his title every year. On great occasions, the king wears a silver-gilt chain about his neck, from which dangles a silver-gilt falcon and he carries a scepter topped by another gleaming bird. In the great hall of the palace portraits of guild kings and head men (club presidents) of the past line one wall. Beneath them stand four ancient cannon no higher than a man's knee, which are wheeled out and fired on the club's anniversary in June and again on Saint Sebastian's Day in January.

Shelves at one end of the room hold silver cups presented by famous members, some of whom were honorary, as was Queen Victoria of England. She gave two cups, the first in 1843 when invited to join, the second in 1893, to mark her fiftieth year of membership. Queen Elizabeth II of England and her husband, Prince Philip, the Duke of Edinburgh, also belong on an honorary basis. Elizabeth sent a handsome cup on her admittance and she and Philip posed for special photographs which they signed and presented to the guild.

One English king was an active guildsman during the two years of exile he spent in Bruges. While Charles II lived in Bruges between 1656 and 1658, under sentence of death should he return to an England ruled by Cromwell, he whiled away many an hour practicing shots in the meadow and the alley of the dark red palace. A spy for Cromwell reported of the king: "He passes his time with shooting at Bruges and such other obscure pastimes." When Cromwell died and Charles returned to rule England, he sent a large sum of money for repairing and improving the guild house; his marble bust occupies the place of honor in the great hall, on the wall above the fireplace.

As you remember, Bruges' commercial greatness ended in the fifteenth century when the River Zwyn was choked by silt, and not only Bruges, but also the towns of Damme and Sluis on the Zwyn, nearer the sea, were changed to inland places. Bruges did not try to reopen a way to the sea until early in the present century, when a canal was begun to a point due north on the coast, called Zeebrugge, or Bruges-on-the-Sea. The project, which included building a harbor at Zeebrugge protected from the silting

action of the North Sea, took eleven years to carry out and was
finished only a few years before the beginning of World War I.
During that war, the Germans used Zeebrugge to shelter their
submarine fleet. One dark night in April 1918, the British bottled up these submarines by sinking three old battleships across
the harbor entrance; their bombardment wrecked port installa-
tions.

After the war, the port was dredged anew; the mile-long break-
water rebuilt. About the time this construction ended, World
War II began. Once more, Zeebrugge was wrecked, so thoroughly
that repairs were not completed until 1951. Now for the third
time in less than fifty years, a canal connects Bruges with a seaport of its own. Zeebrugge ranks as the second fishing port—only
Ostend is more important—and some freighters put in to take on
and unload cargo.

The new canal from Bruges to Zeebrugge bypasses Damme; the
old canal from Bruges to Damme, which once was clogged with
traffic, now is deserted; the shell of a barge drifting on the water
is often the only craft in its entire length. The road follows the
canal, straight and so short that the belfry of Bruges is never lost
to view across the flat green fields. Poplars and willows line the
way, and by the canal where it ends at Damme is the white farm
of Saint Christopher, enclosed by a white, fortress-high wall from
which the white tower of a windmill looks out, sturdy as a donjon.

This once-busy port for Bruges seems asleep; there is no one
in the streets or on the square before the town hall, pretty as a toy
with its end gables, gabled windows in the high roof, turrets, and
statues ornamenting the façade. Several inns have been freshly
painted and look ready to welcome patrons as their signs creak
in the sea breeze; it is the fashion now to drive down from Bruges
for lunch or supper at one of the eating places in Damme.

The inns are open but the church is closed most of the time; its
dark brick walls are crumbling and some have already fallen and
been cleared away; you walk through a passage smelling of decay,

once part of the building, to the cemetery behind the church. Nevertheless, the massive tower has a melancholy grandeur, as befits the scene of two splendid Burgundian weddings. Here in this church of Damme, Duke Philip the Good married his Portuguese princess, and some years later, their son, Charles the Bold, married England's royal Margaret of York.

Yet the greatest name in Damme belongs to a personnage who never lived in the town, who probably never lived at all. Tyl Ulenspiegl was a German and Netherlandish folklore character for hundreds of years before the Flemish author, Charles de Coster, made him the hero of a novel named in his honor, and gave him Damme for a native town. *The Legend of Tyl Ulenspiegl,* which de Coster wrote in French because he did not know enough Flemish, is a piece of Flamingant propaganda. Until de Coster adopted Tyl, the fellow had been known chiefly for rough pranks and nimble wits. Writers down the years had imagined new adventures for him in much the same way as Walt Disney and other authors keep supplying Davy Crockett with new feats. De Coster reformed Tyl, or at least added new and noble traits to his character, made him a loyal Netherlander and put him down in the sixteenth century to suffer and struggle against the tyranny of Philip II and the cruelty of Alva. He turned the scamp into a national hero, but you feel that under the fine patriotic coat, Tyl remains a rogue and a trickster.

The novel is bitter, coarse and cluttered with pages of prophesy and preaching; it is complicated by the author's philosophizing; sometimes the story seems to lie down and die. Yet you read on, fascinated by these men and women of Damme, of Bruges, of Sluis, of Flanders, who gorge on food and drink too much, who betray one another, hate, suffer, love and sometimes are heroic in a world overclouded with superstition and belief in witchcraft. When you have finished, you feel that not Tyl and his friends and enemies but Flanders itself gives the book enduring charm. No one could write of his land with more understanding than de

Coster; he catches the mood of every season: "April when fruit trees bloom"; "May with a clear blue sky and sap turning the branches red"; "September when the gnats stop biting"; "November, the month of rain." He stirs you with the warm spring wind that drives off gray clouds wandering over the sky like flocks of sheep; he chills you in a white world of snow falling on the ships off the Flemish coast, snow which touches the dark water and melts. He helps you to understand the Fleming's love of Flanders, his insistence, sometimes arrogant and overreaching, that it dominate in the Flemish-Walloon partnership.

Damme does not emerge clearly from the story. It might be any small Flemish town. In fact, a French film company making a movie based on de Coster's novel, spent a very short time on location there, because they found that a nearby village lent itself better to the spirit of the story.

13. IN WALLONIA

So FAR, you have been only above the linguistic frontier, and though you may want to see more of the region, it is time to look south and east to the delightful countryside and the cities of Wallonia. Here, farms are larger, villages and towns more widely separated, distances greater than in the north and west, and train service out of Brussels, while still good, is less frequent. For instance, Tournai, though no farther from the capital than Bruges, is connected with it by less than half as many trains a day.

You may decide to go by automobile to Tournai; if so, you will enjoy the trip, for the road is good and runs through interesting country, passing orchards, wide fields and farm buildings about great courtyards, each group looking like a rural fortress even though often painted frivolous pinks and yellows instead of being whitewashed or left the natural red brick. You see more windmills than in Flanders; the sturdy red, white or black towers have long black sails that look delicate as the wings of a giant insect as they idle in the air or turn with the breeze. Now and again, you go by a closed roadside chapel or a shrine with its statue waiting for the prayer of some devout traveler.

Several fair-sized cities give you a glimpse of an ancient town hall or church, of old houses beside a river, and shadowy alleys twisting out of sight. Perhaps you stop in a town to wander through a crowded market on the main square, looking at various kinds of cheese and meat, at blankets, bolts of bright cloth displayed on counters in the open or spread out on the sidewalk; only the men's suits and women's dresses hang under canvas cover.

At the end of a two-hour drive, the five towers of Tournai Cathedral announce the city from far across level fields. This church, one of the largest, finest, oldest—and coldest—in Europe, is architecturally interesting, but most sightseers, who think it striking at a distance, are disappointed on entering it. The massive proportions of the interior detract from the impression of size and space which delicate arches and slender pillars would give. Nothing is delicate or slender inside this cathedral.

After admiring its brilliant windows, you may be glad to go out into the sunlight to explore the Grand' Place, which, although almost entirely destroyed in 1940, has been lovingly restored. Behind the cathedral and separate from it stands the bell tower, the oldest in Belgium. Like the cathedral, the tower escaped the air attacks which wrecked so much of the city. Most of the twelve thousand houses that were destroyed have been rebuilt in the same style as older houses, yet their bright new brick is as depressing as the sight of fresh scars.

Tournai is a quiet place; ordinarily, you see few people in the wide, clean streets or in the parks and gardens. Yet it is busy and rich, with carpet works that export even to the United States and skilled stone masons who carve into statues and baptismal fonts for churches the dark blue stone quarried nearby. Tournai's history is long, complicated and proud. One of the oldest cities in Belgium, it flourished in Roman times on the great road from Cologne in Germany to the sea. Early kings of France were born in Tournai; it was the capital from which they governed their lands to the south and east; several of them were buried here. The tomb of one ruler, upon being opened in the seventeenth century, yielded three hundred golden bees that had adorned his mantle. The idea of the golden bees so appealed to Napoleon Bonaparte that when he made himself emperor he adopted the golden bees as his emblem.

During the Middle Ages, Tournai often belonged to France and it is the only Belgian city ever to have been an English possession. King Henry VIII held it for six years while he called himself "King of France and England."

Earlier, in the fifteenth century, the Tournaisians had supported Joan of Arc's efforts to make the timid dauphin king of France. In gratitude for their help, she invited them to send three representatives to the dauphin's coronation. The story goes that when these delegates returned to Tournai, all their fellow citizens gathered before the cathedral to hear them report on the ceremony, on how Joan looked and what she said and did. When the English took Joan prisoner, Tournai sent her a purse of gold as a token of its affection. The people were always loyal, too, to the king of France, whoever he might be. Nevertheless, they could not be made to fight the enemies of France unless the king himself led them into battle.

In addition to the cathedral and its belfry, King Henry VIII's tower and the Pont des Trous tell of the distant past. The cathedral and Henry's tower have a sturdy air but the belfry and the bridge seem worn-out and fragile. The squat tower, standing in a field near the river, is the donjon of the English-built fortress which was incorporated into the fortifications about the city, and all that remains of Henry's reign in Tournai. It gives the impression of strength even now; its walls are said to be twenty-one feet thick, and grass grows high on the earth covering its rounded top. By comparison, the much older Pont des Trous spanning the river nearby is a mere shell. Yet from the thirteenth century on, this arched bridge, ending on each bank in a square, fortified tower, formed part of the defense belt around the town.

The river, just arrived from France, keeps its French name of "Escaut"; here, before it enters Flanders to become the Scheldt and grow heavy with traffic, it is a narrow, peaceful stream. Only an occasional barge slips under the Pont des Trous; three or four are tied up at the cobbled wharf below the old bridge. Lines of washing drape *Mon Rêve* (My Dream) from Charleroi; a stout woman is polishing the pilot-house windows of *Kamina* from Ghent; a man fishes from the stern of the *Geziena* out of Rotterdam, while *Nord Ster* (North Star) from Hasselt moves down stream, a bargeman's dream with fresh black hull and gleaming white pilothouse trimmed in shiny brass.

Not far from Tournai, just off the road to Mons, is Beloeil, the estate of the Prince de Ligne, a castle more beautiful than the royal palace at Laeken. Its three hundred acres of gardens, often compared with those of Versailles, are laid out in the formal French manner, with clipped hedges and smooth lawns, walks under overarching branches, avenues of purple beeches, paths between hedge walls higher than a man's head and a long lake that reflects the curves of lime trees and chestnuts shading its banks. The castle at the head of the lake is hemmed in by a wide moat; water laps at its rose brick foundations and big carp dart into the sunlight with silver flashes.

The prince and his family allow tourists to visit every part of the castle except their private apartments; the place is truly a museum of rare furniture, tapestries, paintings, books and manuscripts collected by generations of the de Ligne family, which has played a great part in the history of Europe. Although the finest estate in Belgium, Beloeil is only one of countless castles. The province of Hainaut where it is situated, alone contains over a hundred. The government has bought or inherited a few of these picturesque buildings, some in ruins, but the majority are owned privately; often they have been lived in by the same family for centuries. All the castles belonging to the nation are open to tourists, and some of the others, like Beloeil, also admit visitors.

Tournai sprawls over the plain, and the Escaut, or the Scheldt as we call it, is a lazy stream winding through. Two other Walloon cities, Liège and Namur, are built among hills overlooking the more beautiful River Meuse. The view from the heights above Liège is reddened by the fires of blast furnaces and forges, sometimes blotted out by smoky mists, but at Namur, the scenery is still unspoiled. From its fortress on the slope or the open-air theater at the top of the hill, you see the meeting of the narrow River Sambre with the Meuse, and hills that lie along their way.

Around Liège, giant industries make locomotives, glass, guns and steel, and coal miners work deep, dangerous pits. The people of Namur seem proud that they manufacture nothing; they boast: "We are a city of schools and colleges; ours is one of the gayest casinos in Europe. Namur is the gateway to the Ardennes." Liège is a grimy manufacturing city, crowded and noisy, Namur a spotless provincial town, quiet, dignified yet cheerful. Invasions and battles have left neither place with many ancient monuments: at best, an old house here or there, a medieval bridge in Namur, the palace of the bishops in Liège, museums and churches. But both are lively and interesting, and you never tire of wandering through their streets.

You hear Walloon spoken in both cities, more often in Namur than in Liège. A Namur taxicab driver may not know French well enough to explain the sights of the town, or he may speak it with the singsong Walloon accent. Even two young paratroopers from the garrison on citadel hill in red beret and belt seem to be teasing the pretty young clerk in a candy store in dialect. You learn that the Walloon of Namur is not the same as that spoken in Liège. If you remark that in this, Walloon resembles Flemish, which is also broken into local versions, you are told with much indignation that Flemish is entirely different; it consists of many dialects, whereas Walloon is one language, even though the people of Liège and Namur may not understand each other's speech. While you are trying to puzzle out this explanation, some one adds that neither Liège nor Namur use the dialect spoken in Tournai!

A short drive along the Meuse from Namur brings you to the cheerful town of Dinant backed against the cliff. North, south and west of Dinant lie the forested hills of the Ardennes, mountain

streams, ravines and caves, castles and slate-roofed villages clinging to the curving roads. The rain-washed summer air is delicious,
but in winter the Ardennes is the coldest part of Belgium. The
tourist trade is the largest source of income for the region; economists call it a "depressed area" because its industries are few and
small, while the farmland is poor and does not produce much.
The young people of the country go off to find jobs in Brussels,
Liège or Paris, and more of them go to the Congo than from any
other section of Belgium.

Inhabitants of the Ardennes have long been called superstitious,
although the younger generation now denies this charge. Perhaps
they are right; it is possible that people no longer talk of werewolves and children they devour, of packs of infernal hunting
dogs baying on dark nights, of castles and groves haunted by the
devil. Just the same, there is one cycle of legends they will be a
long time forgetting; the Ardennes has prided itself for centuries
on being the home of the Four Sons of Aymon and their magic
horse Bayard, and people will probably always keep on telling of
their marvelous deeds.

Belgium loves the four Aymon brothers, Renaud, Richard,
Alard and Guichard, who have starred in the national folklore
for a thousand years. They sit together on their enormous horse
in every parade of giants through every Belgian city, whether in
Flanders or Wallonia. However, they are natives of the Ardennes
and haunt the banks of the Meuse. The river road near Dinant
passes through a rock split off from the cliff called Bayard's Rock
because the great horse is said to have shattered the cliff with a
single hoof blow when he was carrying his four riders to safety.

Legend says the brothers were nobles at the court of Charlemagne, who had knighted the four of them at the same time. They
had sworn to be his loyal vassals, but broke this oath and like true
Belgians revolted at what they thought was an injustice. With
the help of a cousin, who was a magician, they forced the emperor
to come to terms with them; this exploit alone has endeared them

to the Belgians. Until recently, you could buy in small towns and at country fairs a book printed in big type on coarse paper which told the story of the brothers in very simple words; the work had been popular for three hundred years. Although it might be impossible now to find a single copy of this particular old version of the story, modern authors retell it from time to time so that it is always to be had in some new edition. However, today it is harder to find in a bookstore than *Davy Crockett, Roi du Far West* (King of the Far West.)

Whereas Renaud, Richard, Alard and Guichard are almost wholly imaginary, Godfrey de Bouillon is historical, even though a few extra legends have been draped about his soldierly figure. He was a great noble who, when men prepared to go on the First Crusade, sold his lands and castles and set out with an army of forty thousand followers for Jerusalem, to fight the Saracens who held the city and the tomb of Christ. When the Crusaders captured Jerusalem, they chose Godfrey for its first Christian ruler, although it is said he was too pious to let himself be called king in a city where Christ had suffered humiliation and death. His brother, Baldwin, Count of Flanders, did not hesitate to use the title when he succeeded Godfrey, and Baldwin's descendants ruled as kings until the Saracens finally regained power; the so-called Latin Kingdom of Jerusalem was ruled by Belgian kings.

You are occasionally reminded of Godfrey. You see his statue in Brussels in the square in front of the royal palace—a bearded knight in armor, on horseback, who bears a crusader's banner. Standing amid the bustle and din of the docks at Antwerp you may recall that his grandfather is supposed to have disembarked here from a boat which an enchanted swan had drawn up the Scheldt; legend makes Godfrey the grandson of the swan knight we know as Lohengrin in Richard Wagner's opera.

Nevertheless, the castle of Bouillon in the Southern Ardennes is Godfrey's true monument. The old pile looks down on the pleasant city of Bouillon; it is a romantic ruin with dungeons and broken ramparts where wild flowers grow. It has changed owners again and again, has been often besieged, destroyed and rebuilt, and yet the river below follows the same silvery curves and the view across the countryside is not much changed since the day eight and a half centuries ago when Duke Godfrey rode over his drawbridge for the last time. Now that the castle is ruined and deserted, he seems to own it again.

14. LA CAPITALE

IF you stay in Brussels and go out from it to visit other parts of Belgium, between trips you learn to know *"la Capitale"* as Belgians proudly call the city. You find time to explore the old lower town and the newer city spread on the high ground beyond. You visit the Museum of Ancient Art glowing with the warmth of Flemish masterpieces and the Museum of Modern Art crowded with canvases by later painters, Belgians among them; spend an afternoon in the Congo Museum at Tervueren, the next best thing to a journey to that fabulous land; walk among the elms, the fountains and the statues of the Royal Park near the art museums. You admire the guards before the royal palace; they look very smart in tall fur hats, black coats and white trousers thrust into high black boots. King Baudouin does not live in this town palace, but drives in to it every morning from his suburban castle in nearby Laeken as a business man might commute to his office.

In summer, you drive out sometimes in the evening to the medieval castle of Beersel, not far beyond the city limits, to see a play in the courtyard. If the performance is Maeterlinck's *Pelleas and Mélisande,* then the night, the castle towers and the forest beyond give a fairy-tale atmosphere to the story of a bitter king, a doomed prince and a mysterious queen. Some fine morning, you walk in the Bois de la Cambre, which is really a continuation of the Forest of Soignes, the finest beech woods in Europe; perhaps you row on the lake in the Bois, lunch at a restaurant among the trees or on an island in the middle of the lake. Then, driving down avenues of purple beeches in the Forest of Soignes, you go on to the battlefield of Waterloo, not far away.

You certainly climb the hill from old Brussels to Saint Gudule on the slope leading to the new part of the city. When the church was begun eight hundred years ago, it lay outside the fortifications of Brussels. Its twin towers rose against the sky in Burgundian days, and almost every century since then has added a chapel, a portal, or a flight of stone steps. The entire church was restored in the nineteenth century. Generations of Netherlands rulers have been baptised, married and buried in the lordly aisles and chapels. Here the Belgian people have celebrated victories and sought consolation in defeat. More than once in our own age, under German occupation, the congregation rose and sang with the organ as it pealed out the music of the forbidden national anthem, the "Brabançonne."

The windows of Saint Gudule form a picture gallery of Netherlands rulers from the sixteenth century on; you recognize in the jeweled glass Mary of Burgundy and her Maximilian, Margaret of Austria, Charles V and Philip II as well as Albert and Isabella, the archduchess wrapped in a great red cloak and her husband kneeling nearby. These two are buried in the chapel lighted by their window.

Brussels is sometimes called a "little Paris," but it approaches the French capital's exciting beauty only in the splendor of the Grand' Place with its town hall and guild houses, in the lines of Saint Gudule against the horizon or the bulk of the Justice Building looming on the height above old Brussels. In Paris, the River Seine opens throlling vistas through the heart of town. Brussels' River Senne was vaulted in and paved over eighty years ago because it was an unhealthy, sluggish stream crawling through a maze of dilapidated houses. Today, wide boulevards encircling the lower city trace the river's course under ground; however, the old streets that used to twist down to its banks have not changed their ways—you find them far from beautiful, yet picturesque and interesting.

In the beginning, Brussels was a water city like Liège, Ghent or Bruges. The Grand' Place is said to occupy the site of an ancient marsh. Traffic careens through streets where canals once bore barges. A few street names recall this earlier geography: Firewood Quay and the Quay of Building Stones suggest barges and littered wharves instead of cars parked in an esplanade above a filled-in canal. A house, now a garage, was a cafe beside the Senne for two hundred years and kept its trade even after the river disappeared; people still living recall sitting long ago in its low rooms drinking geuze beer, made from hops and wheat, and eating cream cheese with radishes, a favorite Belgian snack. If you want to see what Brussels-on-the-Senne looked like in those days, examine the paintings hanging in the town hall; they were made just before the river was caged and its slums torn down.

Since no self-respecting Belgian town feels complete without a port, Brussels has one where barges loaded with oil, coal, machinery and manufactured goods come and go by canal between Charleroi to the southeast and Antwerp to the northwest.

Although lacking great beauty, *la Capitale* possesses its own charm. For example, you never tire of the skyline. The tower of the town hall, delicate as the spun-sugar topping to a wedding cake, especially when the Grand' Place is illuminated at night, dominates a welter of dark, Spanish-tiled roofs, domes, slender belfries and jutting gables, with a few television antennas sprouting among the stone or gilded metal stars, birds, animals, ships and statues which decorate the gables. Then there are the chimney pots! Who can forget them, smoking into the low clouds on a gray morning, four or five to the chimney, each pot leading to the flue of a coal stove set up in some apartment or room? Only a few expensive new buildings supply their tenants with central heat.

Sometimes you chance on delightful byways just out of the wash of crowds and traffic: pale, graceful houses dozing about an ancient church or encircling a monument set in a grassy plot, old palaces seen through an archway down a cobbled street, a blind alley beginning with a wrought-iron gate and ending in a tree that branches toward the shabby houses on each side; a ruined tower, last remnant of the city's early fortifications, facing a row of gabled houses.

The most unforgettable park in the city is the Square du Sablon, which tilts its grass and flower beds up towards the statue to the Counts of Egmont and Hoorne, two sixteenth century nobles who refused to join their friend Prince William of Orange, when he fled into the Northern Netherlands to lead the revolt against King Philip II. They preferred to remain loyal to Spain and the established Roman Catholic Church, but they dared to protest the Inquisition and the cruelties of the Duke of Alva. For this, Alva took revenge by having them both beheaded on the Grand' Place in front of the town hall.

Below their statues are others to well-known Belgian scholars and scientists of the same period. However, the most unusual occupants of the square are forty-eight small men in bronze mounting guard at intervals on the railing that encloses it. These figures represent the forty-eight corporations of old Brussels: The baker carries loaves under his arm and a shovel for raking bread from the oven; the miller stands beside a miniature windmill; the artist holds a palette, the fisherman dangles a string of fish.

Brussels constantly reminds you of the part the guilds have taken in Belgian history. The church across from the Square du Sablon was given by the crossbowmen—Charles V is said to have shot down his bird from one of the towers. Almost every other church contains at least one painting, statue or window presented by some guild. The carved and paneled room in the town hall where the burgomaster receives visiting celebrities contains a series of ancient tapestries made in Malines, smooth and bright as oil paintings, commemorating the corporations to which Brussels owes its rise; the dignified figures seem to speak of the pride these craftsmen and merchants took in their community, their trade and themselves.

If you watch the "boursiers" in a downtown hotel, you decide that the medieval guild spirit lives on. The boursiers are an association of business and professional men, not only of Brussels but also, it is said, of Antwerp, Liège and other large cities. In Brussels, they gather once a week for a morning meeting, after which they lunch together according to their occupations. The engineers are at one long table, the brewers at another; here are the rope manufacturers, there coal mine operators. Two wholesale junk dealers sit at a small table by themselves.

Many drift into the dining room after the others have begun lunch; they shake hands with everyone at the table, sit down and order what they want. Soon, the tables are cluttered with food of all kinds and at all stages of the meal: smoked herring and fried shrimps beside apricot tarts, chops near cheese, fried potatoes heaped beside a bowl of fruit, glasses of beer touching pitchers of wine and bottles of Spa mineral water, in the profusion of a still-life by a Flemish painter. The men around the table, their faces flushed with food and bright with talk, could sit for Brueghel or Rubens; you imagine them in the velvets and fur-edged cloaks of their ancestors, feasting against a background of gilt-leather walls in some guild house. By the way, all, even the ruddiest, the most typically Flemish, are speaking excellent French.

The Grand' Place reminds you of the Dukes of Burgundy and their tournaments, but it recalls, too, the archers, bakers, carpenters, butchers, boatmen and brewers who held their meetings and feasts in the lovely old houses that brighten the square with freshly gilded façades. Some sunny day, sit down at a sidewalk table of one of the cafes which, with restaurants, lace and curio shops now occupy the ground floors of most of these houses. This will be a good place from which to stare up at Saint Michael's statue glittering on the spire of the town hall; you will have a chance, too, to watch the flower market spread out under green and red striped umbrellas in the middle of the square. Perhaps you will spot a wedding party emerging from under the arcades of the town hall by the Lions' Staircase, a short flight of steps guarded by two stone lions.

Of course, if you like you may see one or a dozen civil marriages in the town hall. You need only stand at the back of the big room called the Hall of Marriages. On Wednesdays and Saturdays, which are days when the ceremony is performed without charge, the place is full of bridal couples and their friends sitting quietly on long benches, waiting their turn. Ushers in blue velvet coats, knee breeches, black stockings with buckled shoes and fore-and-aft hats stand at the doors or solemnly escort bride and groom to the platform where a city official is to marry them. Each ceremony lasts about ten minutes and consists of questions asked and answered. After it is over, the newlyweds and their witnesses sign the register and, as a new pair takes their place, leave the room by the red-carpeted marble steps leading to the Lions' Staircase. On the sidewalk they stand among relatives and friends, amid kisses, talk, laughter, tears and the click of cameras; then comes the rush of departure in taxis and cars, usually to the church for the religious marriage. If a bride and groom can afford to be exclusive, a fee of two thousand francs, or about forty dollars, permits a car to drive into the courtyard of the town hall to wait for them away from the sidewalk publicity.

Mannekin Pis, the oldest inhabitant of Brussels, has an address a short distance from the Grand' Place, and every foreigner, as well as most Belgian visitors, goes to see him above his fountain. The Mannekin Pis is only a small figure, a baby boy in bronze, whose uninhibited attitude enchants or shocks his visitors. All Belgium shares an amused affection for the little fellow, and he has so delighted some foreigners in the past that they have kidnapped him. English soldiers carried him off once in the eighteenth century, and scarcely had he been returned to his home corner when French troops stole him. This time, the French king sent him back with the title of "chevalier," or knight, and a white satin court suit embroidered in gold. The suit, yellowed by time, is shown with the rest of his wardrobe in a room of the city museum on the Grand' Place. Over a hundred other outfits, which have come from everywhere, are displayed on models of the mannekin or hang from miniature hangers in glass cases. For a Belgian or Brussels festival, you may see him dressed as a bullfighter, a Sioux Indian, an Inca of ancient Peru, a Gille from Binche, a Texas cowboy, a French sailor, a Japanese gentleman or a Scotch laddie in kilts.

One of the nicest things to do in Brussels is to go to the bird market on Sunday morning. It is held on the Grand' Place unless war veterans, a socialist club, a church society or some other organization plans to parade before the town hall; then the market moves deeper into the old town and runs up one block of Christian Man Street and down another of Cheese Market Street. Never have you seen so many birds at one time and from so many countries! There are birds in metal and wicker cages, in wooden boxes! Birds in pairs, by the half dozen! Some of the small kinds by the hundreds. Do you want a canary? A cageful of snowy Japanese sparrows with black eyes and beaks? Wee brown Bengalis with bright red beaks? You will find them here. The cages of small birds are kaleidoscopes of dark green, aqua, purple, black, yellow, orange feathers jumbled with red, yellow, black, pink and red beaks. The big cages hold white cockatoos, love birds and all varieties of pigeons—fantail, pouter, racing.

The market is crowded and noisy. Canaries trill, other birds twitter, dogs bark at each other as they skulk about, men in berets and scarfs, some wearing wooden shoes, inspect the birds, especially the pigeons, and confer in Flemish with the bareheaded, work-worn women who accompany them. Many of these people have come in from the country to look and perhaps buy. They are especially interested in the racing pigeons, because pigeon racing is a popular sport in Belgium. The country is said to have more of these birds than all the rest of Europe. Champions cost thousands of francs, while thousands more are bet on the weekly races. On Saturday, the Belgian radio announces where and at what time the birds will be released the next day by the "conveyors" who have taken them in big willow baskets to the starting point, sometimes as far away as Spain or North Africa. On Sunday, the radio reports every hour on the weather along the route the pigeons must follow in returning to their home lofts. The winner, of course, is the bird covering the greatest distance in the shortest time.

Whether you go to the bird market, a museum, the movies, or for a stroll down a Brussels street, you find the people fascinating to watch, from grizzled old men shuffling along in carpet slippers to clean, nice-looking children playing in a quiet square. The policemen look very spruce with white plastic helmets, white gauntlets and belts contrasting with their dark uniforms. You see numerous groups of khaki-uniformed soldiers wearing a blue, green, red, or white beret and belt to designate their branch of the service; you stop to buy roses or a nosegay of violets from a flower seller sitting under her striped umbrella at some downtown corner.

Perhaps you may just stop to watch the crowds, deciding that nobody here seems to have the time to be lonely or depressed; everyone looks so busy, so intent on the business at hand, whether it is work or fun. The city is thronged from morning till evening, while in the afternoon, the narrow sidewalks of the main shopping thoroughfare of the lower town are so jammed that people overflow into the street. No one seems to mind the frequent drizzle; men walk about bareheaded and unconcerned; the women usually put a plastic covering over their hair and go right on shopping. Only very fashionably dressed women wear hats. If the drizzle becomes a downpour, the crowds take shelter in buildings and doorways, rushing out again the instant the rain diminishes, lively as robins after a shower.

At night, the downtown is thronged with window shoppers, movie goers and people bound for some cafe to spend an hour or so. In Belgium, as in Spain, the cafe is the poor man's club, where he meets friends, reads the papers, plays cards or chess, perhaps listens to a juke box, and often dances; now and then you see a billiard table occupying half the space of a small establishment. The average Belgian would find life dull without the cafe; most neighborhoods are honeycombed with them. One short block in downtown Brussels has six in a row, with two more across the street. In good weather, that is, when it is not freezing or storming, outdoor cafes along the boulevards are packed solid; every table is taken; clients sit elbow to elbow, sipping ices, drinking beer or coffee, nibbling pastries and watching the rest of the city pass by.

15. THE HEART
OF BELGIUM

BELGIANS work so hard that you might expect them to have no zest left for amusement. On the contrary, they have plenty of energy for enjoying themselves heartily. They love parades and celebrations, and go to a great deal of trouble to make these affairs colorful and lively. Even for a braderie, or neighborhood bargain day, streets are hung with guild banners and flags—the Belgian flag, the gold star of the Congo on a blue ground, the Flemish lion, the Walloon cock. There are music and street dancing in the evening.

Every community, from the smallest village to the big cities, commemorates something. Perhaps a new burgomaster is being inaugurated or an old one celebrates his twenty-fifth year in office; the occasion may be the feast day of a popular saint or the anniversary of an event imagined by the local folklore. Whatever the cause for rejoicing, the locality seethes with church services, uniformed and costumed processions to escort the burgomaster or the statue of the saint through the streets, with decorated floats and probably with a family of ugly giants; bands play, local politicians make speeches, the town is illuminated that night while the people dance and the kermis or open-air carnival does a loud and merry business. Some carnivals continue for weeks. In Antwerp, half of April and all the month of May must be hideous for inhabitants of five or six blocks of a handsome residential section.

101

Every inch of parking space on side streets of the neighborhood is clogged with vans in which the carnival people live, while the center esplanade of the avenue is jammed with merry-go-rounds, skating rinks, shooting galleries, dance pavilions, food booths and other attractions that keep up their hubbub until two o'clock in the morning every night of the week.

Brussels celebrates more often than anywhere else, because in addition to ceremonies originating in the capital, every organization in much-organized Belgium seems to yearn to be seen and heard there. Veterans, church societies, folklore associations, boy scouts, university students, labor unions travel in with their banners and bands from Ostend or remote Furnes, from cities as far away as Bouillon or Bastogne, to meet and march through the streets to the Grand' Place. One annual competition, for instance, brings the postal clerks' band from Bruges to compete with the "harmony" (or band) of the railroad men of Louvain, the quarry workers of the village of Quenast who march in wooden shoes, the textile workers from Verviers and the "harmony" of the General Motors Plant at Antwerp. Swinging along, perhaps through pouring rain, the rivals swish their flags and blare out lively airs while the citizens of Brussels stop to listen and watch, unconcerned, too, about the rain.

Fleming and Walloon alike feel the capital belongs to them. The brickmaker from the polder country, the carpet manufacturer from Tournai, the soldier taking commando training at Namur, a professor of the University of Liège think nothing of coming by train or car into Brussels for a banquet, a visit with a friend or a concert. Sports fans flock from kilometers around to see soccer or hockey or tennis, while just as many sports enthusiasts fan out from Brussels to Liège or Mons for other events. Residents of Malines, Louvain, Ghent and Antwerp commute to work in Brussels. Even some of the riders who park a thousand bicycles each morning in the railroad station of Bruges continue by train to school or jobs in the capital.

Realizing that Brussels is the heart of Belgium, you understand why its streets and shops offer every regional feature and all the national products from wooden shoes and famous Val St. Lambert crystal, made near Liège, to Ostend turbot or the "black balloons" of Tournai, candies hard as marbles which Tournaisians think will cure a cold. Brussels tables groan not only with dishes out of French cookbooks, but also with hearty Flemish specialties and characteristic Walloon food. Its shops, eating places and private homes offer almost every delicacy known in the nine provinces—and how many there are! The Belgians eat heavily. More than that, they know and demand good food. Cooks do not spare cream, butter or time in preparing traditional recipes. A working man's family spends a large part of his wages for food—and Belgian wages are high by European standards. It has been said that the government's insistence on plenty of food for the people after World War II was one reason for the country's quick economic recovery, because an austerity regime such as Great Britain enforced would have killed Belgian willingness to work.

Brussels markets display a wide range of seafood; they sell mussels, herring, shrimp, turbot, sole and eels, usually shown coiled about each other like snakes. In season, markets handle everything from larks to wild boar. Among the vegetables you find white Malines asparagus, cauliflower, pale pink carrots no longer than your finger, and chicory or endive. The fruits are luscious: enormous strawberries, cherries, peaches, plums and great black grapes, each bunch too beautiful and almost too costly to eat. What an array of other food in shop windows! Black and white sausages, eels, pickled, stewed or jellied, Flemish *cramique,* a sweet bread yellow with eggs and rich with raisins, gingerbread from Namur and Dinant, called *couques,* which is sold cut and stamped on top to look like ferns, grapes, apples, dogs. If you stand at the counter of one of the milk bars which have grown so popular in Brussels, you may order an American-style hot dog to eat with your milk, tea or tomato juice, but will probably choose instead a big Flemish cake plastered with almonds, or perhaps a slice of rice tart, a custard pie that everyone in Belgium seems to like.

Thirty or forty years ago in the Ardennes, the peasants kept hams smoking in the chimney for use during the long, cold months when they had little fresh meat, but the nation as a whole did not know the flavor of this delectable ham. Now restaurants serve it in paper-thin slices as a special delicacy, but in the Ardennes people still cut it into thick slabs to eat with unbuttered bread.

Chicken or fish *waterzooi* as made in Ghent is on the bill of fare in numerous Brussels restaurants. Chicken waterzooi is fowl stewed with herbs in white wine and butter; the fish variety contains a mixture of eel, carp, bream (a kind of whitefish), cut up and boiled with butter and herbs and spices. Some places serve Flemish *carbonnades,* which are made by braising beef with garlic and onions in beer. Recipes for preparing rabbit or hare vary, but both Flemings and Walloons like it stewed with prunes, the prune juice blended into the gravy. Malaga grapes and little white onions enrich the rabbit-with-prunes coming from Walloon kitchens.

Should you like cinnamon-flavored, thickened cherry soup as the people of Saint-Trond in Limburg make it? Or heavy Flemish pancakes stiff with a glaze of caramelized sugar? What of Flemish carp baked in white wine with onions and mushrooms? Or wild boar chops served with chestnuts? Ham tarts, goose pastries, waffles, cheese tarts? Brussels restaurants or homes prepare all these dainties.

As you go about Belgium, you realize how rarely bird wings flash across a field and that you seldom hear a song trilling through an orchard. The dearth of birds is such that farmers buy large amounts of poison to kill insects which should be destroyed by sharp beaks. This lack results from the national taste for birds cooked in a pie, or some other way. Many thousand times "four and twenty blackbirds" stop "singing" every season in Belgium because not only they, the blackbirds, but also robins, sparrows, thrushes, larks and finches by the millions are netted and trapped, killed and sold to markets and restaurants for a few francs a dozen. Brussels diners consider thrushes cooked Liège style with wine and the flavor of juniper berries a great treat, but bird lovers and farmers are bitter over the slaughter which the government has not effectively checked.

What does Brussels, as well as the rest of Belgium drink? Coffee and tea, much of it imported from the Congo. The tea is well made and good; so is the coffee if you like it strong. Beer ranks with coffee as the national beverage. Belgians drink more beer even than Germans, and all the brewers are said to be rich. For centuries, each locality brewed its particular brand, but now as the smaller breweries are disappearing and large establishments replace them, local specialties have begun to vanish. Nevertheless, you may still have white beer, or black or golden or *kriek*, the ruby-red variety flavored with cherries, bottled like wine and then let stand two years before it is drunk. There are sweetish beers and bitter beers, beer made of hops, and *geuze* which is fermented from a combination of wheat and hops.

You realize what lusty eaters Belgians are when you learn that this nation of beer drinkers also consumes tons and tons of chocolate candy. The capital has nearly as many candy shops as cafes and every small town has its *confiserie* (candy shop). Men and women stand in long lines on the sidewalk before the open-air counters of stores selling cheaper grades of "pralines" as the chocolates are called. You yourself loiter before fancier establishments, tempted by window displays of pralines arranged on silver trays, tucked into gold paper boxes or spilling from toy straw hats. If you go in to buy only a hundred grammes (less than a quarter pound), your small purchase takes a long time to make, because it is hard to decide what you want most from the array of small chocolate baskets with gilt-cord handles, the chocolate leaves, bells, mushrooms, hearts, flowers and tinsel-wrapped mysteries.

Just as Brussels presents a cross section of all Belgian kitchens, so, too, does it share other characteristics of the smaller towns and the country. The national passion for cleanliness is as evident here as anywhere else. Every householder or shopkeeper takes meticulous care of his few feet of living or working space. Whether in Brussels, a Flemish town or a grimy Walloon workmen's suburb, windows shine, curtains have been freshly washed and potted plants are blooming on the sill, the streets and sidewalks have just been scrubbed. You need rubbers even on the sunniest morning if you go walking before half-past nine, for until then housewives and shopkeepers are out washing down the sidewalks. On a wintry day, you wish for a little less cleanliness as you wade through waves of soapy water being sloshed over the floor of the capital's beautiful new central station, which looks as though it had just been opened to the public for the first time ten minutes ago. In Brussels, you could easily see what you saw in Ghent after a heavy storm: two elderly women out in front of the town hall even before the thunder and lightning had ended, sweeping away the rain and pouring fresh suds over the streaming sidewalk.

The Marolles, the rough, working-class quarter of Brussels where many houses moulder in narrow streets, is amazingly clear of rubbish or dirt. Most inhabitants of the Marolles, too, are decently clean all week, while on Sunday they put aside well-worn work clothes and come out looking prosperous and well dressed.

In this connection, a Belgian magazine recently told about an American film company which was making a movie based on the life of the Dutch painter, Vincent van Gogh. Scenes were being shot in Wasmes, a mining town of the Borinage coal region, where van Gogh had been the Protestant minister in 1860. At that time, the living conditions of the underpaid, overworked miners were a national scandal. In the scenes at Wasmes, Kirk Douglas, as van Gogh, was to be shown preaching on a Sunday morning and a number of Borinage residents had been hired to act as his congregation. The American movie director made these extras smudge their faces and wear dark, shapeless clothes, refusing to believe Belgians who told him that on a Sunday morning, even in the Borinage in 1860, people would be clean and decently dressed. Amused and irritated, the author of the article ended: "How stupid to make these people look poorer than they were, and dirtier."

The first pair of wooden shoes you see in Brussels may be a shock to you. But a few days will teach you that they are not merely sold but frequently worn in the capital. Street workers clatter by in them and so do plumbers, pipe fitters, plasterers and other men who work among mud and roughage. Of course, they are more common in the country, especially with farmers, although lacemakers are said to wear them in cold weather to protect their feet from the icy floors when they sit for hours at a time. Newly varnished a bright yellow, the shoes look sturdy enough to last a farmer's lifetime instead of no more than two or three months of constant wear. The wood from which they are made is so soft that the soles quickly scrape through. Of course, wooden shoes cannot be half-soled, but even so it is cheaper to buy a new pair for fifty francs (about a dollar) than to have repairs made to leather shoes, which cost ten times fifty francs when new.

You may not see one sight in Brussels which sometimes enlivens a country landscape—a man in wooden shoes pedaling along on a bicycle. However, Brussels and all the other Belgian cities have thousands upon thousands of bicycle riders. In the smaller towns an even greater proportion of the people use them than in the cities, though nowhere in Belgium do you meet the swarms of cyclists who clog streets and roads as in Holland. You soon understand why bicycle racing is the favorite Belgian sport; every boy feels he may some day be the winner of one of the many tours, or races, which cover the country; there are tours for amateurs, for bicycle-club members, for professionals. When winter makes it impossible for fifteen or twenty contestants to spend a week going over Belgium from one end to the other, then the races are moved indoors to some big sports arena.

The bicycle is a Belgian's work horse, for many, the substitute for a car. You see one parked on a barge; each railroad station has a check room for hundreds left there every day; people of all ages and kinds ride. The delivery boy whizzes about with packages stowed in a wicker basket on his handle bars; a housewife pedals her purchases home in a basket swung out over the rear wheel; sometimes her baby is strapped into a small seat behind her. Young priests in berets and old priests in oval-brimmed hats spin along unmindful of cassock skirts flapping about their knees. But you have seen nothing till you meet a plump nun in the main current of Brussels traffic, wheeling along, her headdress full-blown like sails in the breeze—or gasp at another nun sailing down a steep hill in Namur on a motorcycle equipped with a rear-view mirror on her handle bars.

16. THE LAND
COMMON TO ALL NATIONS

IN BRUSSELS, the cluttered *droguerie* at the corner of the Street of the Swallows and the Street of Flowers sells Kleenex, Palmolive Soap, Gilette Razor Blades and various American detergents, as well as Belgian-manufactured coils of rope, oil for mixing perfumes, strange green powder for who knows what, and wicked black liquid out of two fat glass vessels marked, one "Bedbug Poison" and the other, "Fly Poison." (Droguerie means drugstore, but do not come here to buy cough syrup or aspirin or have a prescription filled; the proprietor will smilingly direct you to the nearest *pharmacie* for all medicines.)

Tractors manufactured in the United States are replacing the Brabant work horses on larger farms, while more than half the automobiles are American made, because Belgians prefer them to European cars. A Chevrolet, Ford or Plymouth never looks so handsome as when navigating traffic in Brussels or Liège, while the larger, more expensive American cars move among bicycles and small French and German models like battleships through a fishing fleet. Belgian traffic is terrifying; even the big cities have few traffic lights and most drivers seem possessed by a compelling urge to "get there first." The country has no examination for a driver's licence; anyone eighteen years old or over may step into a car and try to drive off.

Every road, canal and railway, every harbor and airport admits

foreign goods and travelers. Imports more significant than tooth-
paste, food or machinery flood the country, for Belgium still wel-
comes visitors from abroad and ponders their ideas just as in the
Middle Ages when it was spoken of as "the land common to all
nations." Some newly naturalized ideas surprise you, as when a
young Fleming, after describing the picturesque festivals of his
native region, adds that now they also celebrate two American
holidays, *La Fête de Maman* and *La Fête de Papa*. You are too
taken aback at the thought of Mother's Day and Father's Day on
the long calendar of Belgian celebrations to ask him whether a
procession or a kermis marks these new feasts!

Belgians love the movies and, since they have no companies of
their own, see French, Italian, English and American films; their
magazines and newspapers devote many pages to reviews and crit-
icisms of recent pictures, and the fans know a great deal about
film personalities. Since some four fifths of the pictures shown
are American produced, Belgians feel that thanks to Hollywood
they have become familiar with our way of life. Now and then
an elderly person grumbles about the bad influence American
films have had on Belgian manners, blaming them for the loose,
flat shoes in which young girls scuff along, as well as their pony-
tail hair styles. Other moviegoers are sure Americans live entirely
on coffee, whiskey and sandwiches.

Television is not well developed as yet. The comparatively few
sets in the country—about as many as in one small city in the
United States—have small screens. Nevertheless, people are intrigued by it; you realize their interest when you see the crowds
jamming the sidewalks before "The Voice of the Waves," a Brussels radio and television shop, every time it shows a program in
its window.

Bookstores stock translations of American novels and children's
books in inexpensive editions, but these comprise only a small
proportion of the foreign literature pouring into Belgium, where
French and Dutch works are at home, and English, German and

Italian authors are also widely read. Belgium claims it raises more poets to the square mile than any other country; if this be true, most of them are minor poets, unknown beyond their own frontiers. The Belgian author is, however, at a disadvantage. If his works are put out by Belgian firms, which are small and cannot afford wide advertising, then he may never gain a European reputation. On the other hand, if he has a French or Dutch publisher, he is apt to be considered by most people as a French or Dutch writer.

Libraries in the United States list almost nothing by Belgian authors, either in the original or in English translation, except the works of Maeterlinck and his contemporary, the poet Emile Verhaeren, who wrote with the simplicity and somberness of a Flemish woodcut. Nevertheless, over the last seventy-five years, many Belgian novels and stories have been wonderfully descriptive of life in that country. Such works glow with local color, are rich in details, humorous and lively; they introduce us to unforgettable bargemen, priests, old women, peasants, a butcher trudging from farm to farm to slaughter pigs for Christmas dinners. Their pages open windows on winter landscapes frozen hard as steel or fields softening under spring rain, on a noisy kermis or a rowdy wedding feast at which everyone eats and drinks too much.

Theaters in Belgium, while producing plays by native dramatists, must depend largely on translations of foreign works, and companies from abroad also perform in most of the big cities during the season. You hear good concerts and opera; each important town north of the linguistic frontier has its Royal Flemish Opera House, while Walloon cities hear opera in French. In Brussels, the historic Théâtre de la Monnai (named Theater of the Mint because it stands on a site where money was once coined) gives almost all its operas in French, although now and then it interrupts the repertory to present an English, French or American ballet company. More than once, American Negro singers have sung *Porgy and Bess* at the Monnaie for five or six nights in succession to a full house.

As the daily papers and magazines print many columns of news from abroad, the average Belgian has a good idea of what is going on in the rest of the world; he knows far more about events in the United States than an American learns about Belgium. This is to be expected of the people in a small country centrally located, who have acquired the habit of looking beyond their borders, knowing only too well that what happens out there concerns them also.

Yet in spite of influences from outside, and for all his interest in the ways of others, the Belgian is not Anglicized, Americanized, Germanized or to be mistaken for a Frenchman or a Dutchman. He is stubbornly and typically Belgian. He has had too hard a time for centuries keeping his identity to want to change now. Shrewd, intelligent and industrious, he adopts inventions to make him more efficient, and enjoys foreign ideas and customs which may add to his pleasure and comfort, yet he is far too practical and conservative to imitate anyone. He knows what to take and what to reject and how to be himself.

No people in Europe seem better satisfied at home than the Belgians. In a figurative sense, they work elbow to elbow in their heavily populated country, but they work together and they work hard so that there is enough for everyone. Nobody seems to yearn for wide-open spaces; not even the Congo with its opportunities ever drew many out to Africa. Walloons and Flemings remind you of two brothers who bicker and enjoy life in the family house, which they try always to make into a better place to live.

THE END

INDEX